S. Hrg. 112–390

UNDERSTANDING THE POWER OF SOCIAL MEDIA AS A COMMUNICATION TOOL IN THE AFTERMATH OF DISASTERS

HEARING

BEFORE THE

AD HOC SUBCOMMITTEE ON DISASTER RECOVERY AND INTERGOVERNMENTAL AFFAIRS

OF THE

COMMITTEE ON HOMELAND SECURITY AND GOVERNMENTAL AFFAIRS UNITED STATES SENATE

ONE HUNDRED TWELFTH CONGRESS

FIRST SESSION

MAY 5, 2011

Available via the World Wide Web: http://www.fdsys.gov/

Printed for the use of the Committee on Homeland Security and Governmental Affairs

U.S. GOVERNMENT PRINTING OFFICE

67–635 PDF   WASHINGTON : 2012

COMMITTEE ON HOMELAND SECURITY AND GOVERNMENTAL AFFAIRS

JOSEPH I. LIEBERMAN, Connecticut, *Chairman*

CARL LEVIN, Michigan
DANIEL K. AKAKA, Hawaii
THOMAS R. CARPER, Delaware
MARK L. PRYOR, Arkansas
MARY L. LANDRIEU, Louisiana
CLAIRE McCASKILL, Missouri
JON TESTER, Montana
MARK BEGICH, Alaska

SUSAN M. COLLINS, Maine
TOM COBURN, Oklahoma
SCOTT P. BROWN, Massachusetts
JOHN McCAIN, Arizona
RON JOHNSON, Wisconsin
JOHN ENSIGN, Nevada
ROB PORTMAN, Ohio
RAND PAUL, Kentucky

MICHAEL L. ALEXANDER, *Staff Director*
NICHOLAS A. ROSSI, *Minority Staff Director and Chief Counsel*
TRINA DRIESSNACK TYRER, *Chief Clerk*
JOYCE WARD *Publications Clerk and GPO Detailee*

AD HOC SUBCOMMITTEE ON DISASTER RECOVERY AND
INTERGOVERNMENTAL AFFAIRS

MARK L. PRYOR, Arkansas, *Chairman*

DANIEL K. AKAKA, Hawaii
MARY L. LANDRIEU, Louisiana
JON TESTER, Montana

RAND PAUL, Kentucky
SCOTT P. BROWN, Massachusetts
RON JOHNSON, Wisconsin

DONNY WILLIAMS, *Staff Director*
AMANDA FOX, *Professional Staff*
JUSTIN STEVENS, *Minority Professional Staff*
KELSEY STROUD, *Chief Clerk*

CONTENTS

H605-41331-79W7 with DISTILLER

VerDate Nov 24 2008   10 51 May 17, 2012   Jkt 067635   PO 00000   Frm 3   Fmt 5904   Sfmt 5904   P:\DOCS\67635.TXT   JOYCE

UNDERSTANDING THE POWER OF SOCIAL MEDIA AS A COMMUNICATIONS TOOL IN THE AFTERMATH OF DISASTERS

THURSDAY, MAY 5, 2011

U.S. SENATE,
AD HOC SUBCOMMITTEE ON DISASTER RECOVERY
AND INTERGOVERNMENTAL AFFAIRS,
OF THE COMMITTEE ON HOMELAND SECURITY
AND GOVERNMENTAL AFFAIRS,
Washington, DC.

The Subcommittee met, pursuant to notice, at 10:05 a.m., in Room SD–342, Dirksen Senate Office Building, Hon. Mark L. Pryor, Chairman of the Subcommittee, presiding.

Present: Senators Pryor and Brown.

OPENING STATEMENT OF SENATOR PRYOR

Senator PRYOR. I want to welcome everyone to the Subcommittee. I want to thank you all for being here, and all of our witnesses for being here, and all the interested parties. I also want to thank Senator Brown for being here today, and I look forward to his service in this slot. It may be temporary, but we certainly appreciate you and all that you are doing. It has been a pleasure working with you and your staff on this hearing.

Let me start by just saying that we have two panels today, very qualified witnesses. I certainly want to thank Director Fugate for being here. As busy as he is around the country right now, his time is very precious, and he has been generous with his time and always helpful to this Committee and Subcommittee and helpful to the Senate. So thank you for being here, and all the other witnesses as well, all the ones who are involved in various disasters around the country. We really appreciate all that you all have done and appreciate you being here today.

Last week, a series of severe storms swept across the Southern United States causing immense damage and a historic loss of life. The storm system spurred powerful thunderstorms, tornadoes, and flooding, and it was the second deadliest day of tornado activity in U.S. history, killing 341 people in seven States, including an unimaginable 249 in Alabama. At least those are the latest figures I have. Fourteen people lost their lives as a result of the storm in the State of Arkansas, and I want to offer my most sincere condolences to the families of those impacted or killed during those storms. I hope that your families are comforted through this very difficult time.

(1)

Today the Subcommittee has been joined by very insightful guests to talk about the increasingly important role that social media networks play during disaster response and recovery efforts. From search and rescue to family reunification, to safety updates, to communicating vital shelter information, to other critical or life-saving information, and to all around situational awareness, social media is becoming a tool that people are coming to rely on and to use heavily during emergencies.

In July 2010, the American Red Cross conducted a survey—and they are here today, and they will probably talk about this in more detail, but they conducted a survey of over 1,000 people about their use of social media sites in emergency situations. The results of the survey were striking: 82 percent of the participants used some form of social media at least once a day, and nearly half of those use it every day or nearly every day. The survey found that if they needed help and could not reach 911, one in five would try to contact responders through a digital means such as e-mail, Web sites, or social media.

If Web users knew of someone else who needed help, 44 percent would ask other people in their social network to contact authorities. Three out of four respondents would expect help to arrive in an hour if a call for help was delivered over the Internet; 35 percent would post a request for help directly on a response agency's Facebook page, and 28 percent would send a direct Twitter message to responders.

More than half of the respondents said they would use social media to let loved ones know that they were safe. Their survey also said that respondents with children in households are more likely to use social media, 81 percent, versus 67 percent with those who do not have a child in the house.

As we work continuously to improve our efforts to respond to and to recover from disasters, it is important that we find new and creative ways to communicate information to those facing the often chaotic circumstances that surround emergencies and disasters. I want to thank all of our witnesses for appearing today and contributing to an important conversation that I am certain will lead to more effective tools that will save lives and make delivery of assistance more efficient in the future. Senator Brown.

OPENING STATEMENT OF SENATOR BROWN

Senator BROWN. Thank you, Mr. Chairman. I appreciate the opportunity to serve with you on this Subcommittee today, and as you referenced, my thoughts and prayers go out to those in Alabama and the Southeast who are dealing with the loss of their loved ones and homes this past week.

Clearly, there is no better time to discuss what we are discussing today. I know our witnesses will provide useful insight into the tools and technology that may assist in better response to the recoveries and, unfortunately, future disasters that may be forthcoming.

I actually had an opportunity to go to Google and other types of social media companies to understand what they do and how they do it, and we have met here on Capitol Hill with the Facebook folks and others. And having kids, I understand how they have adjusted and adapted and really learned a lot quicker than me or other members of my family in using social media and related technology. And I have used it quite a bit myself in the last couple of years. So I think it is important to understand how it is being used and what the opportunities for future use are and how we can actually use this when we have natural disasters and other types of situations that we need to get out reliable, important, sometimes life-saving information. I think it is another tool in the toolbox, so to speak, and I am looking forward to the testimony of everybody, and I appreciate everybody appearing today.

Thank you.

Senator PRYOR. Thank you.

Our first witness is the Honorable W. Craig Fugate, Administrator of the Federal Emergency Management Agency (FEMA). He was appointed on May 13, 2009, to serve as Administrator based on his highly distinguished career in emergency management. He will discuss FEMA's short-term and long-term goals for enhanced use of social media tools, and I know that Director Fugate has just come off the road. He has been down in many places, and he may tell us about some of that as well.

We do have a timing system today, and we will do 5 minutes on your opening, and all of your written testimony will be put in the record. Mr. Fugate.

TESTIMONY OF HON. W. CRAIG FUGATE,[1] ADMINISTRATOR, FEDERAL EMERGENCY MANAGEMENT AGENCY, U.S. DEPARTMENT OF HOMELAND SECURITY

Mr. FUGATE. Thank you, Mr. Chairman and Ranking Member Brown. I think Senator Brown said it best. When we talk about social media, we need to understand it is another tool in our toolbox. But it is by no means the only way in which we need to be able to communicate with the public, both in warning and learning situations, but as well as communicating with them.

But I think social media offers a new challenge to us. Previously, we have had the ability to communicate at the public, whether it is radio, TV, Web pages, even billboards that are going up across much of the Southeast where these tornadoes struck, inserts into bills and other things. But our ability to communicate with the public and have two-way conversations has always been limited.

As we have seen in numerous disasters in recent years, we often-times have taken the approach in government of creating systems that people have to adapt to how we communicate. We do not always adapt to how they are communicating. And as we have seen, people began using these tools differently, many of which—or, in fact, almost everything that we use that we call social media was never designed with disasters in mind. But they became increasingly tools of how people were communicating day to day and sharing information with families and loved ones that began providing a role in a disaster in ways that for us in government we did not innovate this. We did not create it; we did not direct it. But we began observing it.

---

[1] The prepared statement of Mr. Fugate appears in the appendix on page 35.

I think for us at the Federal Emergency Management Agency as well as my peers at the State and local levels, as well as the volunteer agencies and other groups that are active in disaster response, we began to see a whole new group of volunteers emerge with skill sets of being able to apply this technology in real-time situations without necessarily a direction from a central location, but more of a term that is oftentimes used of crowdsourcing, many people working on similar problems, sharing information, oftentimes getting to better solutions.

Mr. Chairman, it has caused me to realize that in some ways social media, and particularly volunteers and groups in the industry that are involved in this, I like to put it this way: We need to innovate faster than the speed of government. And they are doing it. And so instead of trying to make systems fit us, make the public fit how we communicate. We at FEMA are trying to meet that need and figuring out how to apply this.

At this point if somebody says Craig, what is the performance matrix? What is the measurement of success? How are you doing this?, I would say we are still experimenting. We are still really just trying to understand how these tools could be applied.

Mr. Chairman, most of the times when we come into these meetings, the first thing you do is turn off your cell phones, hide them and get them out of sight, but I am going to bring mine out because here is what I want to communicate in the short time I have.

In most disasters, when you are displaced from your home, you no longer have access to your computer. You may not have WiFi access. But in many disasters, including being on the ground in Haiti where we had folks there within a day of the earthquake—I was down there a week later—the one thing that was working were mobile devices. And it is this that I think we in the Federal Government need to understand, that we are moving more and more away from a Web-based capacity to a mobile environment.

So one of the things we did at FEMA was to start moving our information into mobile formats. We have a mobile Web page, m.fema.gov, because when you are a disaster survivor, you do not need pretty pictures, you do not need our org chart, and you certainly do not need all of our programs. You need information that will be low bandwidth, that you can go to a phone and get things you need.

We designed our registration so that you could access it by your smartphone. But we are also learning that the public has tremendous information in disaster areas that oftentimes we have taken the approach that it was not official or not usable because it did not come from the traditional forms of communication.

Mr. Chairman, I would suggest that we should look at these as data points, as sensors, that individually may not provide us the best information, but collectively oftentimes are the earliest and best reports of the severity of an impact and are telling us stories faster than any assessment team or any ability to get into an area. We have seen this in Haiti. We saw this in Japan, Christchurch, and even in the tornadoes across the South—pictures, stories, updates giving us information.

I think we need to take the approach in the Federal Government that the public is a resource and not a liability and learn how to listen. But we also need to recognize that we are in a mobile environment, and the Federal Government needs to focus more upon developing the data to support our citizens in a way that they can use in a disaster rather than making them fit our traditional models.

Thank you, Mr. Chairman.

Senator PRYOR. I think those are points very well made and well taken.

Because Arkansas has had so many tornadoes, storm events, and floods in the last couple of weeks—and, again, you guys have been great about being down there and being on the spot, being onsite and helping people—I have been giving out that Web site that you are talking about, the disasterassistance.gov Web site, and your toll-free number. And pretty much everything I have done this week when I talk to Arkansas media, I have been giving that out and encouraging them to do that, because I think that it is just— people just communicate that way today, and you guys can provide such great tools for people to access immediately, and it just is really a game changer. So I appreciate you all being on top of that.

At FEMA, do you all have people in office that are doing your social media focus here? Or is this just part of your overall effort, or do you have to have folks that actually focus on this?

Mr. FUGATE. We do have dedicated staff that are working on what we call digital engagement. Initially, when I got to FEMA, the Web page, using things like YouTube to post update videos, and beginning to do partnerships with Facebook where we would do joint Facebook pages per disaster with the State to share information to the public.

When I got there, one of the things that I asked early on was to begin tweeting, which I had done in the State of Florida, so I now tweet "@CraigatFEMA." I actually do my own tweets. So many people keep asking me, Who does your tweets? I am, like, I do not have staff to tweet, I tweet. And I do not tweet about me; I tweet about things that I think are interesting.

A lot of the people that I communicate with are my peers and practitioners. It is actually interesting. Not only is this useful in disasters, but it is helping build a community in the emergency management that traditionally had to go to course or conferences to see and hear across the Nation ideas. There are things that, when you get into the nomenclature of all of these terms, concept of what a hashtag is in Twitter, what it is, it is something that you build into a message that you can link on that can take—everybody who uses that tag can link everybody else's messages together, so very early emergence in the emergency management community that are asking these very questions about social media applications is a pound sign, social media emergency management (SMEM). That is not led by FEMA, but we have staff that participate.

But this is the conversation taking place with local emergency managers, States, volunteers, researchers, the private sector, and we have never had those kind of—we never saw that interaction outside of conference settings or courses, which was limited.

So we have a centrally directed effort, but it also is underlying some key principles, is give information all the way from high bandwidth to low bandwidth to in-person. We cannot forget there are people who do not use social media. But communicate and provide tools the way people are communicating and using those tools, not limit them to what is just easy for us to administer.

Senator PRYOR. All right. You may not have this available, but do you have examples of how social media has actually saved lives?

Mr. FUGATE. There are examples. I think you are going to have some people in the next hearing that will talk about this. But some of the examples in Haiti where the wireless infrastructure came back on rather quickly, as people were trapped in debris and rubble and you did not have a centralized government system to receive those calls because of extreme damages to both the government of Haiti and to the United Nations, people were able to get out text messages that were being received by people outside the area. They were able to figure out where those people were, approximately, based upon the towers and went back and worked with the cell providers. And I think you are going to hear stories about how a lot of volunteers and people with a lot of technology experience were able to start mapping and providing data in a way that it allowed the United Nations (U.N.) and other forces from the United States Agency for International Development (USAID) to get Urban Search and Rescue (US&R) Teams and other resources where needed. And that was just one example in a country that many of us were kind of taken aback on the devastation, but also the resiliency of the Haitians themselves and how much mobile technology had actually been integrated into their country prior to the earthquake.

Senator PRYOR. And I think back to Hurricane Katrina, and I think about all those folks in the Superdome and other places, and I guess—was the wireless network up and running at that point? You may not know this, but was it up and running in those early days?

Mr. FUGATE. Mr. Chairman, I really do not know, but it is something that—one of the things we have learned in my experience in 2004 and 2005—and I do not know if we have any of the wireless operators that could provide this information. But it has been my observation that the industry learned from those events and how it worked very hard to get in additional resources to both bring back up wireless but also increase capacity. We saw this in the tornadoes where they brought in additional equipment and worked to get cell coverage back up, get wireless back up. And because of that, we have seen—and, again, I kind of look at Haiti as a lesson learned. We actually were assuming until Haiti that wireless communications in areas of devastation would be unreliable and we really would not need to plan for it. Haiti taught me that the industry has learned and is becoming more resilient, and oftentimes it will probably be for many people in the public the first communication that comes back up is going to be the wireless services.

Senator PRYOR. Right. We have a chart here—the second chart,[1] Don, if you do not mind—and it shows Internet usage after four major events, and Haiti is one of those. Then you mentioned Christchurch, New Zealand; Chile; and Japan. And as I understand that chart, the peaks are the top Internet usage, and the valleys

---

[1] The chart referenced by Senator Pryor appears in the appendix on page 93.

are usually at night when folks were sleeping. But you see that they keep using the Internet, and it is a great way to communicate with folks. And like you said, a lot of folks are out of their homes at this point, or they may not have electricity or whatever. They may not have access to their stationary device, but their mobile device they certainly can utilize. So I am glad that FEMA is on top of that trend and is really leading the way in that trend to try to communicate in that way, two-way communication, you are hearing from people, but also you are communicating back to people what they know.

So in some ways, it sounds like social media is the emergency manager's dream because it is such a tool that is so widespread in so many people's hands. Is that fair to say?

Mr. FUGATE. Mr. Chairman, some of my peers now equate the wireless combined with social media as a revolution in emergency management as powerful as wireless was to original public safety radio systems, except now this is far more reaching in the ability to communicate with the public. And so as we see this, again, I think our role here at FEMA is to keep up with the public and not necessarily fall back into what I call innovation at the speed of government, but really look to the technology industry, and as Senator Brown said, I have had the opportunity to go to Google, I have been to Facebook, I have been to Twitter, and really looking into their insights of how we better utilize the private sector as part of the team and not try to re-create things that they do better than us, but use those tools to better communicate and listen to the public as we deal with disasters.

Senator PRYOR. Is it your impression that during a disaster the public will find you using social media? Or do they know where to go?

Mr. FUGATE. No, sir. Again, those people that have had disasters do not, and so this is why we work so hard. And I appreciate every time—this is pretty much the drill, is to get people to register with FEMA, get the information out there. So it is always for us important to get people to know where they can get that information. Part of this is working with the States, things like joint Facebook pages. But I think, by and large, most people are not thinking about FEMA, and that is why trying to build systems that are government-specific tend to fail. It is our ability to use the tools they are using and then direct them to things they are used to using. I mean, if you think about it, when we tell people to go to a Web page that is our typical Federal Web page, it is not easy to find the information in a disaster. That is why we built the mobile page so that when you send them there, it is strictly about disaster information that they need, not, the traditional way that we oftentimes put information on a Web page.

Senator PRYOR. Great. As you are going through this over the next few weeks, I hope you will keep the Subcommittee posted on how many folks are using your page and how that is going.

Mr. FUGATE. We have that, and we will provide that back to staff. You can actually see some of the data of who is using the mobile page, who is using Web pages, versus the traditional calling into the 1–800 number.

Senator PRYOR. That would be great. Senator Brown.

8

Senator BROWN. Thank you, Mr. Chairman.

I appreciate the fact that you have been trying to push out their home page Web page information, and when I was preparing for the hearing and seeing how we could help, our office could help, we are going to actually do the same thing. We are going to put it on our official site in the event of an emergency who you can contact, how you can do it through the various social media or the traditional as well as the new ones, and on our Facebook—I mean, I think I have 250,000—we are going to do the same thing there because I think it is so important to get the information out, because when you are having that natural disaster, you are not thinking about you want to just get in touch with somebody, and you are going to use any mechanism, any phone, land line, shortwave radio, whatever, to help your family and help the people that you care deeply about.

So this hearing and being here as the Ranking Member triggered me to work with my office to develop a plan as to how we can, in fact, get that information out. I would encourage all of us as elected officials to do the same thing.

I noted that the Washington Post stated that people frantically text 911 in an emergency, apparently, and they are unaware that their texts actually go nowhere because in all but a few cases it has not been modernized to actually receive the messages. And people have a lot of faith in 911. I mean, you hear the commercials. We hear regularly, we honor young children regularly for calling 911. But now they text 911.

What are the biggest challenges actually to bringing the emergency services like 911 into the 21st century in your opinion?

Mr. FUGATE. This is a project that the Federal Communications Commission (FCC) is heavily engaged in called Next Generation 911, and it is a recognition that as technology has continued to evolve, it has evolved faster than the original 911 system design. When 911 was originally created, we used rotary dial phones. It was an analog technology. Over time, we have added the ability to give the address and the location and phone number that people were calling from. But then cell phones started to occur, and all of a sudden we realized that all of those phone lines were hardmapped; cell phones are not. And so the industry and the FCC worked to be able to map cell phones, so if you could not tell people where you were but you were calling for an emergency, they could find you with your cell phones.

But now we have, as you point out, people that are using text messages. As the Red Cross survey says, when people text or update or tweet for help, they expect there to be an answer. And this is something that Next Generation 911 is looking to address.

Most likely the first part of that will be text messaging because it would be very similar to a traditional 911 call from a cell phone. The other types of social media are going to take more time, but I think it is a recognition that the FCC—that we need to do that to get that help, but also what it could provide to the responders. And I think in looking at what is done in Europe and other places, oftentimes they have the capability to take live video feeds from people on the scene and give it to the responders as they are en route.

Part of our challenges are 911 was—essentially the architecture and the equipment and the investment was based upon rotary phones and push-button phone technology. And now as the FCC looks at Next Generation 911, how do we incorporate the new technologies and not limit ourselves to just the voice calls?

Senator BROWN. And that is a good segue into my next question, approximately a $9 billion price tag to actually implement those potential changes in a time when we are in a fiscal emergency and dealing with a lot of issues. With Senator Carper, I am on a Subcommittee that deals with fraud, waste, and abuse, trying to zero in on all that stuff. Is there a way not to reinvent the wheel and work with companies like Google and Facebook and Twitter, wherever the social media? I know these entities did not reinvent the wheel and did not start at the base level and then have to spend a tremendous amount of money and maybe incorporate a lot of what is already out there so we can just, add on and potentially save dollars. Is that possible?

Mr. FUGATE. Having served at the county level where I was actually responsible for the 911 system, and knowing that history of primarily the wired telecodes, as the providers of both the technology and equipment, I think this will be one of the challenges as we move forward to Next Generation 911, is to incorporate the other technology players and do that in a way that builds a system that we can continue to enhance without necessarily limiting ourselves to just what we know now.

When we look at the architecture of these systems and we look at where we were and where we are going, it was—we still call them "public safety answering points." It is not a network. It is you dial a phone, it goes to a dispatch center, and then they operate the call from there. And I think a network-based approach like we are looking at with public radio for public safety, looking at network-based radio systems, is the direction that Next Generation 911, and that will open up, I think, a lot more of the technology companies. But I think you are correct in that this has to be done not just what the immediate needs are, but also building a system that we are going to be able to adapt to new technologies that we may—nobody knew about Twitter 5 years ago.

Senator BROWN. Right.

Mr. FUGATE. And so in looking at systems that oftentimes take decades of capitalization to build is how do we build a system——

Senator BROWN. That is adaptable, yes.

Mr. FUGATE [continuing]. That allows us to adapt to the new technology.

Senator BROWN. I know with the storms and everything that has happened recently in Alabama and around the Southeast, when telephone and cellular service is interrupted, what are the Federal Government's efforts to set up mobile cell towers, charging stations, Internet hotspots in disaster zones? And is this part of an SOP in times of major events? Do you have working partnerships with any of the mobile companies to do these sorts of things?

Mr. FUGATE. Yes, sir. This was something that I have been pushing for a long time. Our primary focus with our Federal communication assets has been to get the public safety responders back on the air, and so that will continue to be the priority. But I have also asked my staff to work with the industry that I agree with you, I think it is just as important that we get connectivity back to the public. And you brought up something that I asked our team about, and we are working with industry. We had oftentimes brought in phone banks into areas of devastation so that people could start making phone calls. We have asked and are working on—and I believe I had a report this morning that Verizon is starting this process—is to get cell phone chargers out there.

Senator BROWN. Right.

Mr. FUGATE. So that people can charge their communication devices. And, again, I think this is—oftentimes we tend to be reactive, but, again, it points out the need for looking at how the public communicates in recognizing that, yes, phone banks are good, but, hey, also cell phone chargers for the variety of cell phones is also something that is just as much needed.

Senator BROWN. Just a final thought. I would think that would want to be part of FEMA's, mobile response, a lot of the—whether it is the cell charger units or whatever. So I would just—I am sure they are considering it.

Mr. FUGATE. We are definitely going to be adding that to the toolkit, and it is being implemented as we speak now throughout many of these areas.

Senator BROWN. Thanks for what you are doing. I appreciate it.

Senator PRYOR. Director Fugate, before you run, I just have one or two followups.

I am going to get you to put Slide 1 back up.

One thing you will see on this Slide 1,[1] it is great information, but 69 percent of people out there think that emergency response agencies should regularly monitor their Web sites and social media sites so that you all can respond promptly. I guess the question is: Are we building an expectation here that we cannot meet? And are we monitoring these as we should? Some of this may be State-by-State or even city-by-city issues. But do you want to respond to that?

Mr. FUGATE. Yes, sir, Senator. This is one of the questions that in some cases people are saying should we be doing this because we may create a false expectation. I think, again, as we do this, we are really trying to figure out how is the best way to direct people to the best information, which oftentimes is their local emergency managers and then their State emergency managers, and then what information we provide from FEMA. But we do agree that if you are going to post a blog, we do moderate our comments; we do not necessarily—what we do is we just make sure that whatever comments there are not offensive. But we do not self-censor any criticism. We post it. So the only moderating we do is to make sure there is not offensive material, but we will post the good and the bad and the ugly. And then as we see stuff, we will respond to it.

But we also really need to make it clear that in many cases it is very difficult to have one-on-one conversations. In many cases we are listening to what the community is telling us. And we may not be able to directly respond one on one. So this is the concern and

---

[1] The chart referenced by Senator Pryor appears in the appendix on page 92.

one of the reasons why we make it very clear. If this is an emergency, contact 911, contact your local responders. If this is information or opinions or what you are seeing, we want to look at it. But we may not be able to respond to each one of those postings.

And so these are kind of the challenges. I said, we have to be able to listen to the community, but we may not be able to have that conversation one on one. Yet in one event I actually did. We had a tropical cyclone in the Central Pacific bearing down on American Samoa. I was updating and tweeting out that the forecast, which most people would think would come from the National Hurricane Center, actually had come from the Central Pacific Hurricane Center in Hawaii. I had a person tweet back to me that he was on the island and these were the conditions. And I sent back and I said, "Thanks for the updates. Can you keep sending them?" So we kept using—and we were using the hashtag of the name of the storm, so he kept giving me updates.

And so in real time I had a person that was down there in American Samoa giving me updates about the tropical cyclone. Then it was kind of a—it was almost humorous, but it gave a good sense of what was going on.

Midway through the back end of the storm, he begins tweeting the Chicago Bears/Green Bay game because he was a Packers fan, and I realized that if he is getting information about the game and that was his new concern, maybe the storm was not so bad, and it turned out that fortunately it was minimal damage.

That is a rare example, but it is also very telling of the power of looking at the public as part of the team and a resource and doing a better job of figuring out how to communicate with them. Again, all I was doing was trying to get information out about where the storm forecasts were coming from because this is not something many people were familiar with. But it is just one anecdotal example of how the public can oftentimes tell us more about what is going on than even our official sources.

Senator PRYOR. Right. That is great and thank you for that. Senator Brown, did you have anything else?

Senator BROWN. No, Mr. Chairman.

Senator PRYOR. Director Fugate, thank you for being here today. We probably have some more questions for the record that we will submit, but thank you very much for being here. I know you have to hurry back to do your job, but thank you very much for being here.

Mr. FUGATE. Thank you, Mr. Chairman, thank you, Senator Brown.

Senator BROWN. Thank you, sir.

Senator PRYOR. As Director Fugate is leaving, we will go ahead and set up the table for the next panel.

We will go ahead and set up the witness table for the next panel, and I will go ahead and do a general introduction of folks as we go through this, as they are getting squared away.

Our first witness will be Renee Preslar, public information officer for the Arkansas Department of Emergency Management (ADEM), and she has had her hands full over the last couple of weeks, and she has been a vital resource in managing communications in some of Arkansas's worst disasters. So thank you for being here today.

And, second, we will have Suzy DeFrancis, chief public affairs officer of the American Red Cross. We appreciate you being here, and you guys have been very, very busy around the Nation, particularly in the South, but other places as well, and we really appreciate your time today.

Next we will have Shona Brown. Thank you for being here. She is Senior Vice President of Google.org, and she has spearheaded Google's people operations and business operations groups since 2003. She will share some of her experiences with us today, and we appreciate that.

Then we will have Heather Blanchard, the co-founder of CrisisCommons. She has helped establish CrisisCommons, seeking to connect people and organizations using technology to innovate crisis management and global development. She will detail her experiences with recent disasters as well as emerging trends in the use of social media in emergency response.

So, again, I want to thank you all for being here. Ms. Blanchard, I understand your mother is in the audience as well. Is that true? Good. Thank you, Mom, for being here. We appreciate that very much.

What I would like to do is if we could do 5-minute opening statements and try to keep those to 5 minutes as best as possible, and then we will ask a few questions.

Renee, do you want to go first? Thank you.

TESTIMONY OF RENEE PRESLAR,[1] PUBLIC INFORMATION OFFICER, ARKANSAS DEPARTMENT OF EMERGENCY MANAGEMENT

Ms. PRESLAR. First of all, thank you guys so much for letting us come. I know all of us have been a little bit busy with the storms that have come through the Nation, but we feel like this was extremely important to kind of go through and explain what we do not only from the State's perspective but also from the local perspective, so we can hopefully move forward with the social media presence in disasters.

Arkansas have been using social media pretty much since 2008. We started a little bit with Facebook, but it was not just because it was something new and we thought this was amazing, it was something new we could do. It was because we physically saw documentation where our communities were coming together on these social sites in the wake of disasters, and we realized that, you know what? That was a venue and a media and an audience that we were not reaching directly because we were using our traditional sources, our print, our television, our radio stations. But using online, with the exception of our Web site, as a media outlet and as a tool we just had not done yet. And so we saw that was a vital resource, so we began with Facebook and used it on a preparedness stance before disasters, talking about what you can do. You can get a kit, you can make a plan, you can get prepared. You can stay informed with all the information that is going on.

---

[1] The prepared statement of Ms. Preslar appears in the appendix on page 42.

And we used it a little bit also as a mitigation aspect of disasters, too, simply to show people different projects that they could do to protect themselves in wakes of disasters.

And then after the storms, the severe storms, the tornadoes that came through the positions, we had the tornadoes on February 5, and then we dealt with a lot of flooding in May and March and April and then December I think again. And then we had more tornadoes that seemed—and we saw where there was a need for us to transition from the preparedness and the mitigation side over to response and recovery on the social sites. So socially we began putting out messages on Facebook and on Twitter talking about these specific areas need to take cover. We worked directly with the National Weather Service. They were not on any social sites at that time. So the information that we were receiving from them, we would go ahead and pass along information, too.

In the State of Arkansas, the way that the locals can get the sirens, tornado sirens, things of that nature, it is governed by the local individual jurisdictions. So some jurisdictions use tornado sirens. Some use reverse 911 and things of that nature. But we wanted to make sure that people had an ability to get information from wherever they were going, and that is what we started using, because you might not be in your home listening to the television or you might have satellite television and so during severe weather the TV goes out, and so you need to have an additional outlet to get that information.

So we decided that we would go to them and use that as a tool to go ahead and take care of them making sure that they still got their emergency information taken care of.

In the recovery process it works fantastically because in some areas—all across the State we are dependent upon locals to get our information, the local emergency managers. But when they are dealing with life-saving resources, we go to those local communities that are individuals on Facebook and social media sites to get disaster information so we can then again take it to those emergency managers in their communities to make sure that they can get the resources that they need.

Senator PRYOR. Ms. DeFrancis.

TESTIMONY OF SUZY DEFRANCIS,[1] CHIEF PUBLIC AFFAIRS OFFICER, AMERICAN RED CROSS

Ms. DEFRANCIS. Thank you, Mr. Chairman, and as you said, the recent deadly storms across much of the South and Midwest, including your home State, really underscore the timeliness and importance of this hearing.

As you know, the mission of the American Red Cross is to help people prevent and prepare for and respond to disasters. But today I want to talk about how social media is enabling the public to play a much bigger role in helping us with that mission.

I want to draw your attention, as has been referenced, to a gap that exists today between the public's use of social media in a disaster and the ability of disaster response organizations and relief agencies to act on that information in a timely fashion. And, fi-

---

[1] The prepared statement of Ms. DeFrancis appears in the appendix on page 47.

nally, I want to offer some thoughts about how we can begin to close that gap.

The American Red Cross is a 130-year-old organization, and tools we use to respond have evolved over the years. But perhaps the most exciting innovations are social technologies because they allow us to listen and engage with the public as never before.

We saw this with our fundraising efforts during Haiti. When we rolled out our mobile giving campaign, "Text 'Haiti' to 90999," it was people on social media who really took it viral. In the first 48 hours, there were 2.3 million re-tweets of our text number as people sent it to their networks of followers. And before long, we had raised $32 million via text, $10 at a time, and 41 percent of our text donors were under the age of 34.

We saw the same phenomenon with Japan. The earthquake happened at 2:47 a.m. east coast time, and before most of us even got into the office, our text number was trending on Twitter. Social media communities were way ahead of us in trying to give out ways to help.

But new technologies are not just helping us fundraise. They are becoming part of our operational DNA. In Haiti, we sent out 4 million text messages to the Haitians about the symptoms of cholera and how to prevent it and treat it. Here at home we have built a dynamic shelter map with the help of Google to update our shelter information. We not only have this on our Web site, but we have built an iPhone app so people can find a shelter on their mobile phone.

And we are also helping families connect in those first hours after disaster strikes through our Safe and Well Web site where people can post their whereabouts and update their Facebook and Twitter status.

We are training Red Cross volunteers who deploy to disaster to use their smartphones and social media to let people know where they can go to find shelter, food, and other services. And, really exciting, we are creating a new digital volunteer role where volunteers can help us monitor, authenticate, and route incoming disaster requests without ever leaving their homes.

We know that in a crisis—and it has been said—people turn to the communication tools they are familiar with every day, and disaster response and relief agencies must do the same. You referenced our survey, Mr. Chairman, and we found that more Web users get emergency information from social media than from a NOAA weather radio, a government Web site, or an emergency text message system. Not only are they looking for and seeking information, they are sharing it. One in five social media users report posting eyewitness accounts of emergency events. If someone else is in need, they are enlisting their social networks to help or using Facebook and Twitter to notify response agencies. And, they expect us to be listening.

As you said, 69 percent said that emergency responders should be monitoring social media sites, and 74 percent expect help to come less than an hour after they tweet or post on Facebook. These are extremely high expectations, but, unfortunately, today they do not match reality. Most disaster responders are still not staffed to monitor or respond to the flood of incoming requests during major events.

At the Red Cross, we experienced a heart-breaking situation after the earthquake in Haiti. We began receiving tweets from people trapped under collapsed buildings. We did not have a good way to handle those pleas for help. We had to go through the messages manually and try to route them through the State Department and other places, and in some cases we were too late. These are life-or-death situations, and we must find ways to respond more quickly.

While we will not solve these issues today, we are making progress in collaboration with our partners, as was just demonstrated in Alabama. People affected by the tornado were posting needs to an online gathering point. Working with an organization called "Tweak the Tweet," as well as with FEMA and CrisisCommons, we were able to share that information with the Alabama State Emergency Operations Center (EOC). For the first time, we were able to connect crisis social data with decision makers who can act on it.

I believe you can help us continue to find ways to link up social data with response. We also believe, as you discussed with the Administrator, that the Federal Government does have a role in helping with the Next Generation 911. We agree that the first and best choice for anyone in an emergency is to call 911. However, 911 should be compatible with text and social media.

If I can leave you with one thought, it is this: Social media is enabling real citizens to play a role in helping their neighbors down the street, across the country, and around the world. What we do to help that process will literally save lives and help ensure that our country is as prepared as possible to handle any disaster.

Thank you again for your leadership on this issue, and I am happy to answer any questions you may have.

Senator PRYOR. Thank you.

And now, Ms. Brown, I understand you have a video that you want to show. Is that right?

Ms. BROWN. Yes, I would like to start with a short video, please.

Senator PRYOR. OK. That is fine. If you want to start with a short video, that is great. Are we cued up on that? Sure, go ahead. [Videotape played.]

TESTIMONY OF SHONA L. BROWN,[1] SENIOR VICE PRESIDENT, GOOGLE.ORG

Ms. BROWN. Chairman Pryor and Ranking Member Brown, thanks for inviting me here today and for your attention to this important issue. I would like to apologize for my voice. I am the picture of California health. I oversee Google's efforts to use the power of technology to deliver critical crisis-related information, and this includes the team that develops tools like Google Person Finder, which helps loved ones reconnect during emergencies.

Our thoughts are with the communities that have just been hit by devastating tornadoes, as has already been mentioned, and across the United States which took the lives of, it looks like, over

---

[1] The prepared statement of Ms. Shona appears in the appendix on page 53.

300 people—a stark reminder of the important role of relief organizations. I am here today because we believe technology can make their jobs easier.

In the aftermath of last week's tornadoes, we supported the Red Cross, as already mentioned, by providing maps that located nearby shelters. We updated satellite imagery for first responders, and we directed local users searching for "tornado" or "twister" to the maps through an enhanced search result.

We are not experts in crisis response, and we play a modest role compared to the relief organizations and agencies. But our experiences over the past few years have given us a unique vantage point. In fact, in just the last 4 months, we responded to more crises than we did in all of last year. Based on this experience, I will outline three reasons why simple standard and open Internet-based technologies are critical tools for emergency responders and affected populations. I will also suggest how the government can support these tools.

First, I would just like to tell you about a father who used one of these tools to find his son in Japan. Tom Stormonth's son, Liam, was teaching at a school in Sendai, Japan, when the earthquake struck. Tom was unable to reach his son by phone because the networks were damaged and overloaded. So he turned to Google Person Finder. He posted a picture of his son and asked what any worried parent would: "If anyone has seen him, please let me know he is still OK."

A few hours later, someone responded and said that Liam had taken refuge at a local elementary school. A few hours after that, Liam responded to his father's message saying, "Alive and well." And not long after that, Tom was able to use the Internet-based Skype application to video-chat with his son.

So what makes the Internet so useful following natural disasters and such a comfort to people like Tom? First, the Internet often remains available when other networks fail. In Japan, when other communications systems were unstable, the Internet was uninterrupted. Because of this we were able to get Person Finder up in Japan in only 90 minutes.

Second, during emergencies people tend to turn, as has been mentioned, to simple, standard, and open Internet services that they know well. After the earthquake in Haiti, we sent a team to Port-au-Prince to better understand how relief organizations were using Google tools. Our team was embedded in a refugee camp with the 82d Airborne, and one of the officers explained that soldiers use Google Maps to plan patrol routes for the area because they use tools they are used to.

Finally, the Internet scales and promotes openness. After the earthquake in Haiti, we found there were 14 individual missing person databases. They were not integrated, and they all ran on different infrastructures. We saw an important opportunity to leverage the power of crowdsourcing to create one common database, pushing and pulling feeds from all 14 databases. That idea became Person Finder.

The response has been overwhelming. Person Finder managed more than 600,000 records following the earthquake in Japan, and there were more than 36 million page views within the first 48 hours alone.

Google has the infrastructure to handle that volume with ease, and the Internet remains stable, allowing people to connect. Before Person Finder, Tom Stormonth would have had to go to multiple Web sites and check and re-check in order to try to find news on his son.

In addition, long before the recent flooding in Pakistan, two Pakistani Web developers noticed that available maps of their country were incomplete and inadequate, so they used Google MapMaker to add and update geographical information for millions of people to see in Google Maps and Google Earth. When 20 percent of Pakistan was underwater, we shared our MapMaker base data with UNOSAT, the UN's primary mapping agency, to help them plan their recovery efforts. Similarly, our friends at Open Street Map created the most complete map of Haiti's roads ever made by getting the Haitians to volunteer their knowledge.

What can government do to support these kinds of tools? It can adopt simple, open, and standard ways of publishing and disseminating emergency information. Divergent standards make it much more difficult to collaborate and respond quickly in situations when speed is of the essence.

For example, we have lost valuable time trying to gather and translate into open standards information kept in arcane formats on government Web sites. Also, critical information is sometimes spread across multiple Web sites. And in other cases, important data is not even online at all, but stuck on a spreadsheet stored on somebody's desktop computer.

In particular, alerting systems that leverage the Common Alerting Protocol (CAP), standard could quickly inform users of impending crises such as tornadoes or tsunamis as well as everyday problems like transit delays. If alerts are implemented in an open fashion, governments can provide trusted information, and private actors like Google and others can publish updates that are easily accessible to people when they search for information on their computers or their smartphones. This work can be coordinated with a commercial mobile alert system, for example, so that people have the same opportunity to receive alerts through telecommunications providers or Internet providers.

I would like to conclude by thanking Chairman Pryor and Senator Brown and this Subcommittee for holding this hearing today. We play a modest role, but we are committed to working to help users and relief workers instantly find the information they need during emergencies.

Thank you.

Senator PRYOR. Thank you. Ms. Blanchard.

TESTIMONY OF HEATHER BLANCHARD,[1] CO-FOUNDER, CRISISCOMMONS

Ms. BLANCHARD. Good morning, Chairman Pryor, Ranking Member Brown, and distinguished Members of the Subcommittee. My name is Heather Blanchard, and I am the co-founder of

---

[1] The prepared statement of Ms. Blanchard appears in the appendix on page 58.

CrisisCommons, a volunteer technology community (VTC) that connects people and organizations who use open data and technology to innovate crisis management and global development. Before this position, I spent 7 years at the U.S. Department of Homeland Security, including the position of Deputy Director of the Ready Campaign. On behalf of our community, it is a true honor to testify before you today.

When a crisis occurs, it is not emergency responders who are first on the scene. It is everyday people who use everyday resources like their mobile phone and social networks to share what they know. This could be a road blocked by a tree after a storm or creating a map of where they see wildfires. Today there are many volunteers who leverage technology, like CrisisCommons, that can direct technical capacity, harness open data and collaborative tools to help first responders and communities make sense from the deluge of information that occurs in a crisis. We believe that information at the right time and right place can help response authorities and citizens make better decisions especially in a crisis.

Since the spring of 2009, CrisisCommons has been an open forum to explore how information, including social media, can help in a crisis. Our community has supported organizations and citizens in the response to the Haiti and Japan earthquakes, Tennessee floods, and last week's historic tornadoes which impacted the southeast. Just to share an example, during the blizzard which paralyzed Chicago this year, our volunteers through CrisisCampChicago in collaboration with Humanity Road supported the Chicago Tribune Snow Map to assure that public requests for assistance were routed to 311 and other local authorities.

One challenge that we often see is that government agencies simplify the use of social media as a public affairs function when, in fact, during a crisis access to citizen-generated information is an operational necessity. As an example, this year during our support for the National Level Exercise, the situational awareness work group that we participated in struggled to define how social media information would be coordinated from an operational perspective as there is not a resourced function which connects open data, including social media, and leverages potential surge capacity from communities like CrisisCommons. We would like to recommend to the Committee that government create an operational liaison function which connects volunteer technology communities to our response systems at the Federal, State, and local levels and be resourced for support during steady State and in crisis events. We recommend that current emergency management doctrine be revised to include the capacity to harness technology volunteer expertise and collaborative systems.

Another challenge we have observed is that in local Emergency Operations Centers the connection between social media information and operations is largely absent. We were shocked to find that some centers lacked high bandwidth Internet, technical skills, or collaborative tools. We were also dismayed to find that many agencies have stringent security policies blocking their workforce from using social media tools for operational purposes. Without this capability, emergency managers could be missing critical information in their operational picture. We recommend that emergency management infrastructure be fully modernized. We also recommend that policy and incident management doctrine be modified to allow emergency management personnel to engage outside of their own organizational networks to take advantage of social media tools and capabilities.

As you can see, emergency management may not be prepared to utilize social media tools and data to augment their operations and to inform their mission priorities. When there is a crisis, emergency management continuously find themselves overwhelmed with information. We recommend that resources be devoted toward helping emergency managers with data preparedness and filtering, increasing the level of digital literacy of the emergency management workforce, and empowering their ability to connect with technology support.

In looking at the government's role in this ecosystem, the days of agencies passively sitting on the social media sidelines from behind the firewall are over. The time has come to evolve to a more open and participatory crisis management model. We believe that the Federal Government has a leadership role to play, but, again, we feel that institutional support is needed to move us to the next level. To emphasize we recommend the following:

Create an operational liaison function to coordinate with volunteer technology communities;

Revise policy and incident management doctrine to incorporate social media and other technology capabilities;

Invest in modernization of emergency management infrastructure and collaborative tools;

Support data preparedness and filtering, increasing the level of digital literacy of the emergency management workforce and, again, empowering their ability to connect with technology support.

In spite of these challenges, we know of many emergency managers who are pushing the envelope every day, sometimes at their own professional risk, to apply social media tools and data in their work. We are supportive of the enlightened leadership that Administrator Fugate displays every day. He has opened the door to discussion and experimentation that we see today. However, individuals cannot change institutional challenges by example. Today we are asking for your help to support the needed enhancements that emergency management needs to fully utilize social media information and providing connectivity to communities who can support their efforts just like CrisisCommons.

Thank you very much for the opportunity to testify before you today, and I look forward to answering any questions you may have.

Senator PRYOR. Thank you. I want to thank the panelists.

Senator Brown needs to slip out here in just a few minutes, but he wanted to ask a few questions before he goes. Take as long as you want.

Senator BROWN. Thank you for that courtesy, Mr. Chairman. Thank you.

When introducing the first question, it should be noted that two of our four witnesses are actually public affairs officers, and with that, my question is: How do we start utilizing the tools that we are talking about beyond simply public engagement but to actually informing them of operations and actually respond, in fact, to what is happening? Ms. DeFrancis is probably the best one.

Ms. DeFrancis. Thank you. You are right, we are public affairs. That is where social media sits today. We have a very small crew, two people. If I could introduce Wendy Harman, who is our director of social media and does a fantastic job.

What Wendy and her team are now trying to do is get social media into our own disaster operations center right there at headquarters to make sure that the people who are actually setting up shelters and all that are getting this information and are integrating it. We now have Twitter feeds going on in our disaster operations center to pay attention to this. This is important.

As I mentioned with what happened in Alabama, there are the first beginnings of being able to take this data—and I got to tell you, it does not come in a neat kind of easy-to-read format. It comes in a lot of places, different hashtags and symbols, and it is hard to read. But working with CrisisCommons and other groups, we are trying to understand what are the needs of these emergency operations centers.

In Alabama, they told us to put it clearly: food, water, shelter; organize them that way so we can read them quickly and figure out how to act on them.

So I think, like we said, it is trying to make it part of operational DNA. It is far more than just listening to people. It is really gleaning that information, putting it in a really simple format so that emergency responders, who are very busy at that time, can act on it.

And there are also issues of authenticating it and verifying it, but it is more, I think, getting it clear to them how to use it.

Senator Brown. It must be interesting, too, the language that is used.

Ms. DeFrancis. When we first took in the CrisisCommons data in Alabama to the emergency operations center, they said it looks like a spaceship. [Laughter.]

Senator Brown. Because I know when my own kids send me stuff, I have to call them and say, "What did you just say?"

Ms. DeFrancis. Exactly.

Senator Brown. That being said, where is the potential for more innovation in this area? And what are some examples, if any, of some of the more exciting innovations in this area that have actually taken place so far? Either one. Anybody. It is really for either/or.

Ms. Preslar. OK. There are a lot of places to go, but the first and foremost thing we have to remember is that disasters are local. Disasters do not necessarily happen at the Federal level. They do not even happen at the State level. We are not first responders. It is those people on the ground, our local emergency management offices and things like that. And so I think where the new technology needs to come in is to where we need the government to work with these social companies to create something that our first responders can utilize on a ground zero level. Oftentimes, speaking for Arkansas directly, a lot of the emergency managers in the areas are a one-person staff, and then they rely on their amounts of volunteers that come in and help during those times. But we need something to where they do not necessarily have to have that person that is sitting there 24/7 monitoring the social status of what is going on in these different areas. It needs to be able to work somehow with the companies, because like we had talked before, it was not created for disasters. And now that we see that it is being able to be used and used effectively in emergency response systems, we need to be able to work with those companies to see how we can utilize and kind of narrow it down so we can incorporate it at that local level first and then move up from there.

Senator BROWN. And, Ms. Brown, if I could ask you a question, I know—and I appreciate the video and everything Google is doing. The impact of disaster response and the dedicated crisis response team that you have, is this a full-time group within Google?

No. Press it again.

Ms. BROWN. I am failing Microphone 101, obviously.

Senator BROWN. That is OK.

Ms. BROWN. Yes, we have a dedicated team that is based in Mountain View and New York. However, it is important to note that when a crisis occurs, it actually brings together, in addition to that team, a lot of Googlers who otherwise have other jobs. For example, in Japan, we are fortunate to have an office there, and so it was not difficult to have a lot of people drop their current activities and literally live in the office day and night, certainly for the first 4 or 5 days. So we supplement that core permanent team as needed with resources around the world. But it is a permanent team based in the United States.

Senator BROWN. Was there any specific philosophy or reason for Google to set up that dedicated team that you saw a need and you wanted to go in and zero in or you wanted to be a leader in the area? And with that, do you see an expanding capacity and dedication of additional resources in this area in the future?

Ms. BROWN. In terms of why it entered the area, I mean, quite simply it was an area consistent with Google.org's philosophy of an opportunity for us to take some of our technology and deploy it for social good. We did not spin the roulette wheel and pick crisis response, but it looked like something where, quite frankly, information and communications are critical, just, of course, as food and water are after a disaster. And we seemed very well positioned to help around communications and information.

In terms of increasing our resources, it has grown over the last couple of years. Actually over the last year, since Haiti, we realized the power of it, and at the moment the team is continuing to respond to natural disasters and continuing to focus on making the tools more applicable and scalable.

So, for example, when there is not a disaster happening—which has been small windows of opportunity this year, unfortunately. But when there is not one, they are actually working on, OK, what sorts of data might we aggregate ahead of time so we could respond faster and so on.

Senator BROWN. Thank you.

Ms. DeFrancis, is there any area where you may need Congress' help in legislation to streamline, consolidate, make better, more efficient, anything like that, that you or anyone else maybe can think of?

Ms. DeFrancis. Senator, if I could respond just quickly to your last question about innovation, one of the things we are learning— I mean, none of these tools were available back during Hurricane Katrina—Twitter or Facebook. And so here we are 5 years later. Then we think, well, what is the next 5 years? So I would say whatever solutions that we all are working towards, we need to be careful not to tie it to one particular application or technology because they are changing so rapidly.

I think in terms of the help we need, I think just holding this hearing is really great because it raises the prominence of these issues so that people begin to think about them, begin to work around them. We are having great success working in collaboration with FEMA and other government entities. As Heather said, Administrator Fugate has been terrific in that regard. We are working with all of these groups here, Senator, and Twitter and Facebook, and I think there is kind of a crowd mentality that comes together with this medium. And so I am not sure that I think government should jump into the middle of it or try to interfere with what is happening. But I think that there are places where probably government is needed to provide the resources, and we mentioned the emergency 911 as one of those examples and bringing together wireless companies to do that.

Obviously at the Red Cross we will need to continue to invest in new technology. We want to get this where it is not just a manual thing, where we have to have people monitoring every second, but where it begins to become a stream that is automatic, that goes into the right places in these operations centers. We will have to invest in training——

Senator Brown. Can I just ask kind of a followup to that?

Ms. DeFrancis. Yes.

Senator Brown. Not to interrupt, but is there a point where it is too much information? It seems like it is overload. You have a crisis. Everyone wants to do the right social thing to help and be helpful. At what point, though, is it, like, OK, we get it? How do you draw that line?

Ms. DeFrancis. Yes, Senator, I think it can be overwhelming, and that is why we are trying to find the common standards and ways in which we can feed this information so it just does not all come in at once in different ways. I think Heather is working on that. Heather, I do not know if you want to address that aspect.

Ms. Blanchard. Sure. I think that when we talk about information overload, what we are really talking about is a lack of filters. You really need to be able to look at the body of information. It is kind of like a river, if you will, and the river is flowing. And during a disaster, the river is overflowing. And what you really need is filters.

And a lot of times those filters really operate based on data standards, and data standards is something that is really important in this area. And the question is, like in an operations center, who is sitting in the seat that is creating the filters for that information? And so being able to kind of have that eye for the kind of information that needs to come in to be able to augment the operational picture to better make decisions for the people that— from the incident manager all the way up to Craig Fugate. And I think that there is a common misperception is that—there is a term called "common operating picture," and in a way, like what you really want is a user-defined operating picture, because what an incident manager needs to see on the front lines is very different than what Craig Fugate needs to see. But they need to be able to have access to the same pool of data. So open data is really important. It is really the backbone of what we are talking about. And social media is information that becomes points of data. So if you have a tweet and that tweet has—you turn your geolocation on your phone, well, that tweet can be mapped now. But a lot of times people when they tweet, they do not have their geolocation on their phone, so we cannot say, OK, here is a damaged building unless they give you context to say it. But if they did not give you any context and they have their geolocation on, we can automatically pull that into a map, and that gives emergency managers better information.

Senator BROWN. Thank you, Mr. Chairman, for holding this hearing. I appreciate the opportunity to participate.

Senator PRYOR. Thank you.

Senator BROWN. Thank you, everybody.

Senator PRYOR. Thank you for being here today. See you Monday.

Thank you all for all your testimony. Let me dive in with a few questions. I actually have about 10 pages of questions. I am not going to worry about—— [Laughter.]

But I do have several questions, and in the interest of time, I may submit some for the record. I do not really know where to start, so, Ms. DeFrancis, let me just start with the Red Cross. Something you said in your testimony—everything that you all said caught my ear, but something you said in your testimony that caught my ear is in Haiti the Red Cross sent out 4 million texts to people, which I think is a great tool and a great resource. I am curious about how you got all those phone numbers to text, and also I am curious about do you have that capability in the United States with various privacy concerns, et cetera.

Ms. DEFRANCIS. Thank you for that question. In Haiti, cell phone use is incredible. I think it is like 90 percent of the people in Haiti have cell phones. And as they were going into these camps and tent areas, we were registering them. We actually piloted a program to see if we could actually give money to families through their cell phones so that they would go to a particular place, a disbursement place, and get money right into their hands so that they could provide for the needs of their families.

So there we had people going into tent communities where they were registering, and that is how we were getting those cell phone numbers and were then able to push out the right information.

To be perfectly honest with you, Senator, I do not know that we have that capability right here in the United States. It is certainly something that we are looking at. I know that certainly emergency management agencies are looking at that. But, when a crisis strikes, the first thing you grab is your cell phone or your car keys. And so to be able to have that ability to push that information out would be terrific, and maybe that is an area that we can all work together on.

Like I say, I know government is working on some of the things, but we at the Red Cross do not have all those phone numbers by any stretch.

Senator PRYOR. Did you have any success with your pilot project about texting people some sort of voucher or a code where they could then go get money?

Ms. DEFRANCIS. Yes.

Senator PRYOR. Did that work?

Ms. DEFRANCIS. It worked in the pilot phase. For a number of reasons, the Haitian Government decided, at the end of the day, that was not the best thing to do. But we certainly think that it will work in future operations because most people are familiar with where to go to a bank or something. You will get a code through your cell phone, you will be able to take it to the bank, and, immediately, the bank can verify that and give the money to you. So it is a very fast way to do it, and there is kind of a synergy here between people who are now texting to give money to help people and people using their cell phones now to be able to take that and get that immediate help.

Senator PRYOR. All right. You mentioned in your testimony also the Alabama experience where you guys have had a lot of success there using social media, and it seems to be working well and it seems to be fairly well integrated. What steps do you have to do to set that up? Or does it just happen spontaneously?

Ms. DEFRANCIS. Heather is probably more the expert on this, but it happens pretty spontaneously. What happened was that a personality in Birmingham set up, kind of, a Web site and said, "Hey, send me all of your needs." He was a radio personality right?

Ms. BLANCHARD. Yes.

Ms. DEFRANCIS. And so people began to text all their needs. And they are everything. They are everything from, "I need baby food, diapers," things like that. Someone needs tree removal at their home. Others, shelter, a church is setting up a shelter, they need volunteers, they need, diapers, these kinds of things. And all these needs started pouring in. And, so what the emergency operations center said was, "Can you begin to put those into a more orderly catalogue so we can digest it and then get the help?" But, really, these things grow up organically, and people are looking at that site to say, "Maybe I can go run some diapers over to that site. I am nearby." And that is great. We want to encourage that. That is really neighbors helping neighbors.

Senator PRYOR. Ms. Blanchard, did you want to comment on that?

Ms. BLANCHARD. Sure. Part of the project really, the genesis of it, the Red Cross had come to us, and also Humanity Road is a nonprofit that utilizes technology to also be able to take information and be able to help people in crisis. There were two projects, one, again, with the emergency operations center and the other was Tuscaloosa News. Tuscaloosa News actually launched a Crowdmap, which is basically an open platform where you can actually take pieces of public information like Twitter, and it can go on a map. And so we heard of that project and this project, and what we wanted to do is merge the projects. And so now we have probably about 50 volunteers associated with another organization called the Standby Task Force. And these people are all over the world, and they are basically combing the Internet right now as we speak to find needs that people are saying in Alabama. And so they are taking that information and they are cataloguing it and they are putting it on the Crowdmap that Tuscaloosa news had generated. Crowdmap is a product of Ushahidi, and Ushahidi is an open mapping platform, and that is the platform you saw that was deployed during Haiti. It was also deployed during the Japan crisis that we just saw earlier this year.

Part of what we see is that a lot of times a Crowdmap is deployed, but Crowdmap may not be exactly the right tool because you really need a full instance of a Ushahidi platform because you are dealing with a lot of load, a lot of information, a lot of customization that needs to happen behind the scenes.

And so we recommended to the Tuscaloosa News and to the Red Cross, hey, let us get together and see if we can kind of put this in a platform that will really be able to work long term. And so right now we have volunteers working basically around the clock, and we are actually reaching out to local universities to see if they want to host the platform long term to make sure that we have local grassroots engagement on it.

So what the platform seeks to do is it seeks to pull in all the needs that people are talking about, and the local EOC is going to look at those needs. The people that are planning in the planning section, and they are going to be able to say, OK, we are planning that these folks over here—we have feeding stations in this town, but we are seeing on Twitter that people need food. We want to make sure that we are closing the divide, closing the gap. And so in a way they are using it to double-check their planning and operations, which is really fascinating.

So we are really happy to support the Red Cross, and we are also really happy to support Tuscaloosa News, and we are really hoping to be able to help them over the next coming days.

Senator PRYOR. Is it fair to say that in what you are doing, the larger the disaster, the larger the need? Because with the larger disaster, there is more devastation and more of the sort of local systems go down and more people are impacted. Is that fair to say?

Ms. BLANCHARD. It is fair to say, but I will give you something that is really great to see. In a way, the biggest the disaster, the more that people really want to help. And sometimes there are really large disasters all over the world that people do not even know about. And so what has really been amazing is that we have seen this rise of what we call the crisis crowd. So a lot of times people talk about the wisdom of the crowds and people being able to use crowdsourcing.

What we have seen and really what Haiti demonstrated was this massive ability for people all around the world to connect to each other using basically the global platform of the Internet and being able to work on common projects. Like missing persons, that is a really great example. Missing persons that became—after Hurricane Katrina, the community of volunteers got together and created actually their own technical standard because there was no technical standard that was available. And so they actually felt, well, no one is creating it, we are going to create it. So that is what created the People Finder Interchange Format (PFIF) Standard, and we would be more than happy to submit more information about that. And that evolved—during Haiti, that evolved into basically a lot of technology volunteers that had experience during Hurricane Katrina came together and said, hey, there is a data standard that is already available, and Google was able to take that data standard and actually create their missing persons database based on that.

And so now for CrisisCommons, what we are trying to do is that later this month we are actually holding a missing persons data summit in Paris to be able to kind of work further on privacy issues, being able to figure out how people can be able to better utilize this information.

So there are lots of different pieces, but the crisis crowd during every crisis really wants to respond, and what we really want to kind of look to see is like how can we make the response smarter. How can we make, getting information to a map for local needs quicker? How can we have—for example, during Alabama, you were talking about categories. What if we had predetermined categories? We do not need to even think about it. We just go. And so that information, that river of information could go ahead and flow into a map and be able to really automatically provide information that is critical to emergency management.

Ms. DeFrancis. And, Senator, could I just also add, on the local front, though—you talked about major disasters. As you probably know, at the Red Cross most of the disasters we respond to are house fires, and they do not get a whole lot of coverage. But what we are discovering, through our chapters, who are also now tweeting and using Facebook, is that we are able to bring the local community—make them aware that this has happened down the street, and that these are neighbors of theirs who need help.

And so I think it does not just have relevance for the big ones that get all the media attention, but it also has relevance for the everyday emergencies people go through.

Senator Pryor. Right. So, Ms. Blanchard, let me ask you—I want to talk about the mission persons program or application that you offer. How does someone in Tuscaloosa find out about the availability of missing persons—or someone in Utah, for that matter, wanting to find someone to make sure they are OK in Tuscaloosa, how do they know that is out there? How do they know that exists?

Ms. Blanchard. So there is actually—coming from—being at DHS for over 7 years, I really kind of got familiar with the emergency management protocols, and during disasters in the United States, the Red Cross is the lead for missing persons, and we really seek to support that. But there are other efforts such as Google's missing person finder, which is great, because that really condenses the amount of missing persons databases that currently are created.

So when there is a crisis, a lot of people create well-meaning technology tools, like missing persons databases. And what Google did during Haiti was able to collapse those down basically into just one that was able to really be propagated all over the Internet, which was really helpful. But I think that when you talk about if you have a missing persons—if you have a family member that is missing, the American Red Cross is the place, and the Safe and Well is what FEMA asks people to go toward. And we want to support the local response efforts.

Senator PRYOR. And, Ms. Brown, tell us about the need for universal data formatting. I mean, I think I understand that, but tell me sort of in layman's terms what that means.

Ms. BROWN. Is that working? There we go. Good with databases. Bad with microphones.

So PFIF, which is the standard that Heather was referring to, was, as she described, created out of the genesis of the Haiti experience and is a standard that we are continuing to iterate on today. But the concept is essentially that if you receive data, rather than as Suzy was describing it is a spaceship and all sorts of different order, it would be an order with a field name that you would understand. So everybody would call something "first name" as opposed to "family name" or "F name" or something. And so that would mean that when data was coming in, it could be interpreted, and you can have actually different databases easily talking to each other. That is the premise.

Ms. BLANCHARD. Yes.

Ms. BROWN. So if everybody made the word "data" compatible with PFIF, then the speed with which everyone could talk to each other during a crisis and, therefore, as an end result the speed with which someone could be looking for something and be able to look into a whole bunch of different data sets rather than just one silo here and one there would be dramatically increased.

So that is the basic idea of the data standard.

Senator PRYOR. And so are most people on the same data standard? Or are they all over the board?

Ms. BROWN. No, not most, but increasingly there are.

Do you want to comment, Heather?

Ms. BLANCHARD. Yes, we are very much promoting the active use of the PFIF Standard, also with basically data interoperability.

Senator PRYOR. Right.

Ms. BLANCHARD. Making sure that different databases can talk to each other. And today, like, that is definitely able to happen.

Senator PRYOR. OK.

Ms. DEFRANCIS. And, Senator, could I just add? We are not the Missing Persons Bureau, but during a disaster we do obviously register people in our shelters, and then we take them to our Safe and Well Web site and make sure they post there.

But what we are really about with all these technologies is kind of like Craig Fugate said, let us not try to fit people into our systems, let us try to work with the other systems. That is why we became compatible now with Facebook and Twitter. We are working with Google on People Finder. Because whatever is the easiest way for that person, that is the way we want to go. It is not proprietary Red Cross, Safe and Well. It is not proprietary. But can we all work together so we get this data together and get help?

Ms. BROWN. And just to your question about who is using it, I mean, for example, in Japan, we did find that many organizations did use this standard, particularly the police, and so when you are talking about missing people. But you need more organizations using the same—you need all these organizations that identify people to be using the same standard for it to work perfectly, and we have a ways to go.

Ms. BLANCHARD. And the great thing is that everyone here is actually—we have monthly calls on missing persons data, and so we have been trying to create some kind of continuous improvement processes on that. So we are sharing information, and we are looking at the standard, and we are hoping to be able to contribute something meaningful to it.

Senator PRYOR. Ms. Preslar, let me ask you a question about Arkansas and the specific experience you have had in the last few weeks in our State with all of our storms.

Do you feel like that our citizenry and the various government entities are using the social media effectively? Do you feel like we are sort of following this trend that some of these other folks have talked about?

Ms. PRESLAR. It is very diversified across the State. You will find in the urbanized or the areas closer to the urban—central Arkansas, there is a large group of people that actually do utilize this. In northwest Arkansas, there is a large group. There are some in the northeast centered around Jonesboro and then some around Texarkana. And then everywhere else across the State, Fort Smith included, it is just kind of scattered. People may use it, people may not. But I think that also has to do with the fact that you see the areas that it is followed around right now. It is also the areas that have a large media center. You have the television stations and things that are localized around there, so you have people that they can follow.

I think that is why I stated earlier, when we talked about getting groups of people or getting companies together to decide how we can actually use this for emergency management in mind will help the local areas, because when you have smaller counties that do not much less have a budget, much less, an actual county government Web site, social media provides them that opportunity not just to do things during the response and the recovery phase, because before you can do that, they have to know where you can go to get that kind of information, and that is where the preparedness phase steps in, is that when you have your local emergency managers utilizing this stuff in advance of a particular disaster, during that disaster people know where to go to ahead of time, and that is why it is so important that we go ahead and work on that obviously ahead of time to make sure that we can get that together, we can get that set in place. And I think that you would see a lot more involvement once the individual emergency managers at the county level that do not obviously have a budget much less, full-time status are able to do this without any, Web training or Web experience or know how to do any type of HTML coding. They can pretty much enter things into specific sites via a blog that is already laid out for them or a Facebook account that is already laid out, where they can just put in the information and they do not have to worry about how that information actually gets to where it is going.

Senator PRYOR. Right. And you are at ADEM.

Ms. PRESLAR. Yes.

Senator PRYOR. The Arkansas Department of Emergency Management. Do they have a designated person for social media? Is that you?

Ms. PRESLAR. "Designated" is very loosely defined.

Senator PRYOR. Right.

Ms. PRESLAR. Yes, I am the one that does it, but it is not my sole responsibility. It does fall under the public affairs staff of the side of things where it belongs, and there are two of us on staff, and I am the one who handles the social media things. In fact, actually tomorrow we are training additional staff to be able to make sure that it is timely and it is congruent and that we are not just involved in social media when I am awake. [Laughter.]

We are trying to make sure it follows the timeframe, and we are actually doing some of that training tomorrow. So we do have someone that does take care of that stuff, but it is important for it to be done on all aspects and all levels. In the State's Emergency Operations Center, I will sit in and I will monitor things as they come in, and then I will go out and directly talk to the people that are positioned in the EOC that deal with the counties on a first-name basis to where, if I see something is coming through for Prairie County or I am getting reports that roads are flooded and they are concerned about an evacuation, I will go to that event manager that is in the EOC that is going to be discussing things with the Prairie County emergency manager to make sure, OK, is this true, is this going to happen? Because like we said before, the emergency managers are so consumed with their life-saving responsibilities, which is where they need to be, but they do not necessarily have the time to come back to the State and say, OK, this is going on now, and this is going on now, and this is going on now. So to be able to have that additional side where we see what the citizens are saying or maybe what the citizens are receiving, we can say, OK, they are actively getting the message, and they are getting the message effectively. OK, this area does not seem to be getting the message that the county wants to display, so we need to figure out how else we can best get this information to that local community.

Ms. DEFRANCIS. We saw that a lot in Alabama, sir, where people would say, "I am in this particular area"—I think it was Hackleburg—and "We do not have any food, we do not have any water." Well, they did. They just did not know where it was. So social media allowed us to put out to them. "Well, no, go to the corner of X and Y and that is where you will find it."

Senator PRYOR. It seems to me that also something we have not talked a lot about today is the local media, especially the local TV stations in our State, and probably the newspapers and radio as well. But the local TV, because we have had such bad storms, say they pretty much would just discontinue their normal programming just do weather all the time as these terrible storms are rolling through. But it seemed like they were getting a lot of social media information as they were covering this.

Ms. PRESLAR. Absolutely.

Senator PRYOR. I think that helps bring awareness to some of this as well.

Ms. PRESLAR. Like I said before, we use it as a tool not only to get information out to our public, to the citizens of Arkansas, but also to get information out to that media standpoint. On a public affairs side of things, especially in a disaster, by the time that you put out that initial press release, it is already old information. It is already delayed, and you have already got the new information that came in while you were going through the sector to get the original one approved.

The way the media puts the expectations of all responsibilities in getting information out, social media allows us to put out a simple statement within roughly 15 minutes of something happening. Even if that is simply stating, the Arkansas Department of Emergency Management and the State of Arkansas has activated its State Emergency Operations Center; we are monitoring what is going on; as we get information, we will give it to you. It lets citizens know and taxpayers know, OK, the State is not doing nothing, they are doing something, and we know that now. Whereas, before, they had to wait an hour or 2 hours to get that potential information. And even though the message does not really change, it justifies and I think it validates the fact that they know that people are doing something about what is going on .

Ms. DeFRANCIS. We actually have observed that if something is on Twitter or trending on Twitter for about 24 to 48 hours, the next jump it will make is to CNN. So it is definitely happening, both mediums.

Senator PRYOR. Right. Let me ask a Federal, State, local government question, and that is on budget. Does social media cost money? Is this adding to your overhead?

Ms. PRESLAR. Not at this time. But at the same time, in me saying that, we are very limited in what we actually do at the moment. It could justifiably cost money. When you talk about the opportunities that there are out there for, the mapping purposes—and mapping is excellent, especially when we were just so recently talking about a potential New Madrid earthquake. An earthquake of that level, of that intensity that could happen, being able to map things like that through social media would provide instant information and a source of information—roads, bridges, gas lines, fires, things of that nature—where it might—we are discussing still how are we actually going to get into these affected areas. But if people are able to have that capability inside, that would affect it.

Obviously a lot of these things can cost money. Actually, analyzing what is coming in and using analytics to determine, OK, which of your messages are being effective, which of your messages are not being effective, and how do you need to rework the ones that are, are not being out to the audiences that you need. It can cost money. At this time, we have not spent a dime on it, but we have always got places that we can go to make it improve where we currently stand. But at the same time, without spending a dime, I think that we have very effectively used what we have been able to take care of.

Senator PRYOR. Right. Ms. DeFrancis, let me ask you—I am going to put up Slide 3 here, which is a pie chart,[1] and it is about your survey. I would like to know a little bit more about the survey. As I understand it, you asked 1,000 people around the country. How did this work?

Ms. DeFrancis. Yes, as I told you, during Haiti this was the first time we were sort of stunned by the fact that we were getting tweets from people trapped under collapsed buildings, and we had no way to answer them. So we decided we wanted to convene a summit on all of this, which we did last August. But in advance of the summit, we wanted to be informed as to how much the public really is using social media, and so that was the genesis of the survey. We surveyed about 1,058 Web users, so these are people who are already pretty well on the Web. But I think, like you said, we are seeing a huge—we would love to do the survey again each year and see where this is going, because we expect that it is growing and that more and more people are turning to it.

We are also seeing demographically, obviously, we are seeing younger people using it more. But as they get older, then it will become more the way that people operate.

So it was very useful in giving us a baseline, if you will, for how social media is becoming such an important player in the disaster space.

Senator Pryor. Good. That is helpful.

I actually do have a lot more questions, but in the interest of time, I think what I will do is submit those for the record. But I would like to finish with one just general question, which kind of goes back to the mission of this Subcommittee, and that is, I would like to get your thoughts on what, if anything, the Federal Government can do to help make the use of social media more effective, more available, more accurate, just a better tool for all of us to use before, during, and after these events. And your answer could be the government needs to just stay out of the way and let this just happen. If that is the answer, then that is a fine answer. But I am curious about your thoughts on what, if anything, the government can do or should do better.

Ms. Blanchard, do you want to start?

Ms. Blanchard. Sure. I actually think that government can do a lot, and I think that the private sector has definitely a huge role to play, but I think government always takes a really great leadership position. The government has different types of mechanisms such as advisory councils. FEMA has a national advisory council. It would be really great to see a technology committee on that. In addition, to inventory the resources that could be brought to bear, to support local and State authorities. For example, being able to provide imagery, aerial and satellite imagery, during disasters so you can do remote disaster assessments, and you can actually harness technology volunteers to be able to do that. So just being able to inventory a lot of those assets.

The other thing is that the Federal Government does data really well, NASA and NOAA, the Weather Service, I mean, there are some really great agencies that work with data all day long. In a way, being able to share their lessons learned just as it is applied to emergency management I think would be really helpful.

---

[1] The chart referenced by Senator Pryor appears in the appendix on page 94.

Again, data standards is always something I know that FEMA is working on. A couple of crisis data standards, that would be helpful.

Guidance, I think it would be also helpful, and then, of course, looking at the grants, because, we definitely want to build capacity so you do not have kind of a—it is great that you have one super star person, but you really need—in a way, it is not the technology tool. It is the data behind it, and it is the people that are behind, being able to coordinate that information across not only public affairs but also in an operational sense.

Senator PRYOR. Ms. Brown.

Ms. BROWN. Thanks for the question. I will keep it simple, which is to say I think that if the Federal Government were to encourage all of its agencies and bodies to use tools that are simple and standard and open, that would really be helpful in all the ways that it can do that.

For example, NOAA as well as USGS have been using in their alerting mechanisms the Common Alerting Protocol and that is terrific. And if everyone used the same protocol as per our earlier discussion, then our ability to be helpful to the government on aggregating for alert purposes would be immensely enhanced. So that is one example, but there are many. And simply encouraging that behavior in all the ways that it can would be most useful.

Thanks.

Senator PRYOR. Ms. DeFrancis.

Ms. DEFRANCIS. Thank you, Mr. Chairman. We struggled with social media at the Red Cross when we first broached it because we did not know how we could control it. I guess in a way it is a medium that you cannot easily control. As we discussed here today, it is very organic. It is people/citizen input coming in. So I am not sure that we would see government stepping in to set standards or come up with hashtags or things like that, because it seems to be a much more fluid type of medium.

I do think that by drawing attention to the issues here, I do think there will be resource issues, particularly, as Renee was talking about, with local and State governments who are trying to staff emergency operations centers and have the technology and have people trained. There may be issues there of how can they afford that, and certainly we have already discussed that with the new Next Generation 911 there are issues there, too, because even if the FCC were to say here are the rules, you still have to resource local and State governments that have their own 911 systems. So there may be a role for grants as well in this area.

But I think what you have done today by convening the various organizations and groups and drawing attention to this problem and this opportunity is really important.

Senator PRYOR. Thank you. Ms. Preslar.

Ms. PRESLAR. I have said it several times already about the importance, and I cannot stress it enough we would like the Federal Government to work with these private companies on how social media platforms can be created to allow the responders to utilize it in an operations standpoint, and then from that have toolkits that those local emergency managers would be able to use fairly easily, and then the guidelines—because it always gets back to guidelines and regulations, but allow those to be flexible enough to allow the new technology to work instead of having to continuously go back and edit legislation and guidelines as the new technology becomes available, just allow it to be able to be flexible enough in the beginning that it can go ahead and integrate into the system.

Senator PRYOR. Great. I want to thank you all for being here, and like I said, we are going to have some more questions for the record. We had a couple members that could not make it today.

We do want to thank you all for being here, and we are going to leave the record open for 2 weeks, and again, thank you for changing your schedules and making time to be here. And if you have ideas as you all continue to do what you do, please do not hesitate to let us know because it helps us understand what is going on out there, and, maybe we can prod the Federal Government to do better in some areas and to allocate more time and attention and resources to this.

So, again, thank you for your time, and I appreciate all that you do, not just here today but all that you do around the country to help save lives and put this country back together after a disaster. Thank you.

[Whereupon, at 11:47 a.m., the Subcommittee was adjourned.]

A P P □ □ □ I □

Written Statement of
Craig Fugate

Administrator
Federal Emergency Management Agency

Understanding the Power of Social Media as a Communication Tool in the Aftermath of Disasters

FEMA

Before the
Senate Committee on Homeland Security and
Governmental Affairs

Subcommittee on Disaster Recovery and
Intergovernmental Affairs

Washington, DC

May 5, 2011

□3□□

I. Introduction

Good morning Chairman Pryor and distinguished Members of the Subcommittee. My name is Craig Fugate, and I am the Administrator of the Federal Emergency Management Agency (FEMA). It is an honor to appear before you today on behalf of FEMA and the Department of Homeland Security.

I am particularly pleased to be here today to discuss the role of social media in disasters and emergencies. Technology grows and changes rapidly. Tools that did not exist even five years ago are now primary modes of communication for millions of individuals. Of course, tools like YouTube, Facebook, Twitter and others were not created for the purpose of preparing for, responding to, or recovering from emergencies and disasters. However, our success in fulfilling our mission at FEMA is highly dependent upon our ability to communicate with the individuals, families and communities we serve. For that reason, social media is extremely valuable to the work we do, and we are fortunate to have partners in the social media community with us here today who see the value of using these tools to increase public safety.

In my testimony today, I would like to discuss why social media is important to the work we do, what social media tools FEMA uses in order to fulfill our mission, and what the future might hold for the nexus between social media and emergency management. We at FEMA greatly appreciate your interest in this important subject.

II. The Importance of Social Media in Emergency Management

FEMA's "Whole Community" approach to emergency management recognizes that individuals, families and communities are our greatest assets and the keys to our success. In order to fulfill our mission, we must recognize that the public is an important participant in the emergency management community and that we must work together as one team. The notion of treating the public as a resource rather than a liability is at the heart of our emergency management framework.

Communication in and around a disaster is a critical, life-saving part of FEMA's mission. Social media provides the tools needed to minimize the communication gap and participate effectively in an active, ongoing dialogue. Social media is an important part of the "Whole Community" approach because it helps to facilitate the vital two-way communication between emergency management agencies and the public, and it allows us to quickly and specifically share information with state and local governments as well as the public.

However, it is just as important that these parties be able to share information with us. I often say that individuals, families and communities are our nation's 'first' first responders. The sooner we are able to ascertain the on-the-ground reality of a situation, the better we will be able to coordinate our response effort in support of our citizens and first responders. Through the use of social media, we can disseminate important information to individuals and communities, while also receiving essential real-time updates from those with first-hand awareness.

2

Most importantly, social media is imperative to emergency management because the public uses these communication tools regularly. Rather than trying to convince the public to adjust to the way we at FEMA communicate, we must adapt to the way the public communicates by leveraging the tools that people use on a daily basis. We must use social media tools to more fully engage the public as a critical partner in our efforts.

III. FEMA's Social Media Tools

FEMA uses multiple social media technologies to reach the public where they already go for information and provide valuable disaster and preparedness information. Social media platforms are valuable tools in our toolbox. While no individual tool is exhaustive or all-encompassing, each allows us to communicate with the populations we serve – before, during and after a disaster occurs. I would like to discuss a few of the social media tools we use at FEMA, and how we use them.

Official FEMA Channels on Third Party Sites

FEMA utilizes the resources of several non-governmental social media channels – such as YouTube, Facebook and Twitter – as tools to communicate with the public. On FEMA's Facebook page, our more than 33,000 followers can receive updates on current situations and get preparedness tips through text, photos and videos. We also post information in Spanish.

On FEMA's YouTube page, users can watch videos detailing FEMA's response and recovery efforts, along with clips on topics such as how to prepare a disaster kit, what to do and where to go in an emergency, and how to apply for disaster assistance. The same videos are available on www.fema.gov.

FEMA's Twitter account offers brief updates to those looking for disaster preparedness or situational updates, including tweets in Spanish. FEMA also uses sixteen different Twitter accounts, including:

- A main FEMA account (@fema);
- My account, which I update regularly (@CraigatFEMA);
- The Ready Campaign account, designed to educate and empower Americans to prepare for and respond to emergencies (@ReadydotGov);
- Citizen Corps, which helps coordinate volunteer activities that will make our communities safer, stronger, and better prepared to respond to any emergency situation (@citizen_corps);
- U.S. Fire Administration, which provides national leadership to foster a solid foundation for our fire and emergency services stakeholders in prevention, preparedness, and response (@usfire);
- The Louisiana Recovery Office, servicing Louisiana communities recovering from Hurricanes Katrina and Rita (@femaLRO);

3

- Each FEMA regional office also posts on its own Twitter account, providing localized information on FEMA activities.

Twitter users can also follow topics of conversation that are of interest to them by following a "hashtag," which is the name given to a common topic of conversation on Twitter. The Social Media in Emergency Management hashtag (#smem), while not created by FEMA, allows all members of the emergency management community to connect and talk, including emergency managers at the federal, state and local levels, technology volunteers, private sector entities and interested individuals. I am an active participant in the #smem conversation.

In order to facilitate further discussion, FEMA created the #imprepared and #kidsfiresafety hashtags, and in partnership with the American Red Cross, created the #howihelp hashtag. The #imprepared hashtag is used to encourage individuals and families to get prepared; the #kidsfiresafety hashtag is used to encourage parents to practice fire safety tips; and the #howihelp hashtag is used to encourage people to talk about how they help their neighbors and communities.

While YouTube, Facebook and Twitter have different capabilities and audiences, we use each of these tools as a way to facilitate two-way dialogue with the communities we serve.

Finally, last year, FEMA signed an agreement with Google Books to make FEMA publications available in a free, online format. Many FEMA publications are also be available through Google Books to e-readers, allowing the public to read FEMA publications in a portable format. We continue to look for new ways to use technology and social media to eliminate barriers to communication between FEMA and the public.

www.Challenge.gov

One of the ways we treat the public as an emergency management resource is through www.challenge.gov, the federal government's platform for soliciting public input for creative solutions to government challenges. Between October 2010 and January 29, 2011, we accepted ideas for innovative and effective ways communities can prepare for a disaster before it strikes. We posted over 150 submissions from the public, and will promote the winning idea on the FEMA website in the coming weeks. Individuals and state and local governments can also view the submissions, providing one more mechanism for sharing ideas and best practices across the emergency management community.

FEMA's Presence on the Internet

The FEMA homepage is frequently updated to provide the most relevant and up-to-date information to the public, prominently displaying preparedness information, links for disaster assistance, and updates on any ongoing situations.

In December 2010, FEMA also created a blog (www.blog.fema.gov), which provides information before, during and after a disaster strikes, and highlights the best practices, innovative ideas and insights that are being used across the emergency management community.

4

Ready is FEMA's personal preparedness campaign. Through its website, www.ready.gov, *Ready* is designed to educate and empower Americans to prepare for and respond to all emergencies, including natural disasters and potential terrorist attacks. The goal of the campaign is to get the public involved and ultimately to increase the level of basic preparedness across the nation.

FEMA's Mobile Website

In early 2010, FEMA launched its first-ever mobile website, which allows the public to view our easy to load web pages directly on their smartphones. The mobile site features information on what to do before, during and after a disaster, along with the ability to apply for federal disaster assistance directly from your phone. As we witnessed during the response to the Georgia and Tennessee floods in 2009 and 2010, disaster survivors often have little with them but their phones. As a result, providing the ability to register for assistance from smartphones enables us to immediately mobilize the appropriate assistance to support our citizens' needs during disasters.

IV. What's Next for Social Media in Disasters

While we have greatly improved our ability to communicate with the communities we serve by tapping into new technology and social media, we cannot stop there. Over the past two years, I have met with representatives from Apple, Craigstlist, Facebook, Google, Microsoft and Twitter to continue the discussion on how we can harness the ever-changing capabilities of the digital world to better serve the public. While we have come a long way, we must continue to change and evolve the way we do business. We can do this in several ways.

Plan for Mobile

Cell phones are data centers, capable of quickly accessing and storing a large amount of information. Cell phones are continually gaining new capabilities, providing internet access, the latest weather, and access to our favorite social networking sites. For these reasons, cell phones are a lifeline during and after an emergency.

One of the major lessons we learned from the January 2010 earthquake in Haiti was that even if the physical infrastructure of an area is completely destroyed, the cellular infrastructure may be able to bounce back quickly, allowing emergency managers to relay important disaster-related information and enabling the public to request help from local first responders.

The fact that individuals are likely to have their cell phones on them in a disaster environment is highly relevant to how we must plan for disasters. FEMA's mobile site is an important step in the right direction, and I encourage my state and local counterparts to create mobile versions of their websites that are easy to navigate from smartphones, allowing the public to receive localized information during a disaster. In particular, we learned that text messaging was a key communication stream during Haiti. Survivors were even sending information on their locations via text – this proved helpful for everything from search and rescue to commodities distribution centers.

5

State and Local Participation in Social Media

We also continue to encourage state and local governments to engage with the public via social networking sites. Many states and localities are already taking action, and we are happy to support those efforts. For example, in the aftermath of the 2009 flooding in Tennessee, we worked with the Tennessee Emergency Management Agency (TEMA) and set up a joint Facebook page that we used as a resource to provide the public with the latest information about ongoing disaster response and recovery efforts in Tennessee. Now that the main recovery phase has concluded, TEMA uses the Facebook page as its own means to share preparedness and disaster-related information.

Receiving Valuable Input from the Public

We value two-way communication not only because it allows us to send important disaster-related information to the people who need it, but also because it allows us to incorporate critical updates from the individuals who experience the on-the-ground reality of a disaster. The exigent nature of emergency management makes time a critical resource. The sooner we are able to comprehend the full scope of the disaster, the better able we are to support our citizens and first responders. For that reason, we must seek out and incorporate information provided by the public.

This means that we must incorporate relevant information from all sources – including government at all levels, volunteer groups, the private sector, and also the public – in order to produce what we call a common operating picture. We must integrate public input and move away from a government-centric approach to emergency management. I have challenged my governmental and private sector partners to "free the data" by making non-sensitive disaster-related information like evacuation routes and shelter locations available and accessible to the public, so we can share the best information we have for decision-making in disasters. FEMA also looks at how we can view this information geospatially by plotting it onto a map, in order to improve our situational awareness during and after a catastrophic event.

A New Kind of Personal Preparedness

I have often said that a commitment to personal preparedness among the individuals, families and communities we serve is one of the most important keys to our success. Traditionally, that has meant doing things like having an emergency kit and a plan to reunite with one's family, and that remains important. However, cell phones and social media have created new ways in which individuals can prepare themselves for disasters. A family or personal communication plan for disasters might include the following:

- Store useful phone numbers in your phone, including local police, fire departments and your utility company;
- Create a group for your emergency contacts on your cell phone;
- Know what social media tools are available to you at the state and local level, so that you can quickly access them in the event of an emergency;

6

- Have an extra battery for your phone (or a solar charger) in your emergency kit;
- In the aftermath of a disaster, update your social media channels to let your friends and family know you are safe by simply saying "I'm OK." This helps reduce the volume of phone calls in an area so that necessary communications can continue to be made.

Personal and family preparedness is extremely important regardless of the disaster. However, as technology grows and changes, so will the ways in which individuals and families must prepare for disasters.

V. Conclusion

At the heart of all of our preparedness, response and recovery efforts is our strong belief that as members of a community, we bear the responsibility for ensuring the well-being of those around us when a situation demands collective action. Similarly, being able to rely on one another for help in a crisis makes our communities closer and stronger. It is that interdependence that makes two-way communication in a disaster so important.

My pledge to the individuals and communities we serve is that rather than asking them to change the way they communicate to fit our system, we will continue to change the way we do business to fit the way they communicate. In doing so, we will not only reach the largest possible audience to share important information, but we will help facilitate a two-way communication, engaging the individuals, families and communities as a critical part of our emergency management team.

Thank you again for the opportunity to appear before you today. I am happy to answer any questions the Subcommittee may have.

7

MS. RENEE PRESLAR

Deputy Public Information Officer
Arkansas Department of Emergency Management

TESTIMONY

Before the Senate Homeland Security and Governmental Affairs Committee
Subcommittee on Disaster Recovery and Intergovernmental Affairs

Understanding the Power of Social Media as a Communications Tool in the
Aftermath of Disasters

May 5, 2011

Arkansas Department of Emergency Management
Building 9501 Camp Joseph T. Robinson
North Little Rock, AR 72199

Introduction

Thank you Chairman Pryor and distinguished members of the Subcommittee for the opportunity to testify today regarding the use of social media as an effective communication tool in disasters. This is a critical topic and the recent storms throughout the South have brought the use of social media during weather events to the forefront.

The Arkansas Department of Emergency Management (ADEM) has been using social media since 2008. Like others, our agency is tasked with disaster preparedness, response, and recovery of the State of Arkansas. Social media has worked as an effective communication tool for ADEM as it has enabled ADEM to capture important messages for citizens of Arkansas on sites they already use.

ADEM began with Facebook, primarily as a preparedness tool, using it to educate Arkansans on disaster preparedness. ADEM then expanded its audience by utilizing YouTube. In the fall of 2008, a personal Twitter account was created by an ADEM's Public Relations employee. The Twitter account was created to determine whether Twitter could be a social site for ADEM to consider. During the ice storm of 2009, it was noted that the public used Twitter, among other social platforms, to obtain disaster related information. Information on the site gave the public road openings/closings, shelter location/availability, and energy outages. At that time, it was determined ADEM should have a presence on the site and similar sites.

It was determined Arkansans were utilizing social sites and would benefit from information that ADEM was sharing with media outlets. ADEM expanded to Twitter in 2009 with the Mena tornadoes and utilized the social media tools for communication. With the use of the social sites it became easier to get essential information to citizens. Rumor control became easier now that we had established a presence on the sites and the public would refer rumors to ADEM for validation. ADEM used social sites to communicate directly with disaster impacted citizens, families of impacted citizens, reporters, and volunteer organizations. Media outlets began retweeting ADEM's messages which allowed for an even larger audience to be reached. ADEM noticed the social media's full potential as a crisis communications tool.

Those in the emergency management field often say that a nation, state, and community are only as prepared as its citizens; and it is true. Social media has enabled the state and local emergency management agencies to prepare their communities by bringing preparedness information to them.

ADEM encourages local Offices of Emergency Management (OEMs) to engage in tools their communities are using. When time and resources are limited, emergency managers need make use of primarily tools that their audiences employ. Of the citizens that utilize social sites, the majority are found on Facebook and some on Twitter. Social sites have given local emergency managers a site to post disaster related information and interact with their communities without website development knowledge required.

Preparedness

Arkansas uses social media as a tool to make preparedness information available to citizens. Examples of ADEM messages include, tips on preparing for disaster, scheduled preparedness events, and training opportunities. Creation and communication of preparedness messages before a disaster is significant. Creation during a disaster only assists in the preparedness for the next one.

ADEM also uses the Facebook page as an opportunity to illustrate to Arkansans that state agencies collaborate by sharing information sister agencies, local emergency management offices, as well as other states' emergency management agencies.
In a disaster, the question is always asked, "What did you do in advance to prepare Arkansans for this?" Using social sites is one way ADEM educates individuals on the importance of self preparation.

During National Preparedness Month 2010, ADEM and the Arkansas Chapter of the American Red Cross teamed up on Facebook and Twitter to issue daily messages on preparedness. This partnership enabled delivery of messages to Arkansans in a medium that allows citizens to respond with questions and/or comments, as well as share disaster related information with others.

Local OEMs make use of social platforms in the same fashion as state agencies. Social media sites, such as Facebook, assist local OEMS in locating citizens who offer their assistance in disasters.

Social media sites help communities stay involved with local emergency management. A Facebook page allows communities to understand the extent local OEMs go to in order to keep their communities prepared. Rural areas may not have much as far as media is concerned and some local governments have limited resources for a website. If one exists, it may just list basic contact information. Having a virtual location where the county emergency management office can post what is going on in their community; the steps it takes for them to be prepared; the actions that they take during a disaster; and places the community can go to get trained...it all is involvement. When the time comes that a citizen needs help they are going to know where to get it. And if they specifically are not on these sites to see this information, chances are someone they know is.

Lastly, we use it for preparedness because social media gives us an opportunity to directly communicate with our audience. While we still use traditional media outlets; it is no longer our only option. If questions or rumors come up, we can not only go to media outlets to help answer and correct, we can also answer them directly.

Response

Social media has become a huge asset during the response phase of disasters. It provides the capability of putting information out as we get it. Often in response, by the time public affairs has gathered information, written a release, and received approval to distribute, the message released is not the newest information available. Incorporating social media into our communications plan allows us to keep the public up-to-date as information is available.

Like in preparedness, this does not mean we stop traditional media and press releases; it just means we now have an ability to stay on top of the audiences' expectations. ADEM tries to develop and issue an initial statement within 15 minutes of being made aware of a situation. Social platforms allow us to not only reach the media within that time frame, but reach Arkansans directly. Having a constant flow of information in short bursts lets citizens know the State is working. Responding within 15 minutes of an incident saying, "ADEM is monitoring the XXXX and is ready to assist counties with whatever resources are needed" is enough in the beginning for Arkansans to see the State is doing something. Would we write a press release with one sentence? No, but it is acceptable to write a one sentence message on social sites. As the situation continues, it allows the public to receive information as it happens.

ADEM uses its social sites during the disaster response phase: keeping Arkansans up-to-date on weather watches and warnings (at least the information on where to find the alerts); reporting areas with damage; assisting locals in evacuation notices, rumor control; monitoring what is going on across the state; answering individual questions from citizens.

Online it is important for everything to be linked together to create order. Having data available is great, but until we know what to do with the data and until our audience is able to put data together, it does not become a usable message. Making our data searchable is a great way to ensure that when our audience is looking for information, they will find it.

One way ADEM has created order in monitoring Twitter is by setting pre-established hashtags. In January of 2010 we polled our followers on Twitter and asked what hashtag they would like to see for the upcoming winter weather – we wanted to establish something in advance to have some order to the data we monitored. As suggestions came, we realized we could create one hashtag for all weather related events. In doing so we could narrow our monitoring responsibilities down considerably. Instead of attempting to track everything anyone in the state of Arkansas was posting as individual events, tornadoes, ice storms, floods, severe weather, drought, we could follow it all by using one designated hashtag. After all, we did not want all the data that was out there, only what was relevant to Arkansas weather. #ARwx was created for the simplicity of working for all weather events in the state of Arkansas. It also happened to be only a few characters long so most messages aren't affected by its presence.

We involved our followers in the creation of our hashtag for one reason. Social media is all about community involvement. In order for our hashtag to be a success it had to be used. A large part of the #ARwx success is due to the fact that ADEM did not push a hashtag on anyone, but instead went in the direction the Arkansans wanted. Once #ARwx was created we publicized it. Messages were sent out before potential weather events reminding people to use it.

Meteorologists also joined, as well as storm trackers from all over the state. Currently it stands as a valued resource for Arkansas weather information. Not only has it gained the attention and use of current Arkansas twitter users, but also national media outlets looking for our state's severe weather information through twitter. We are also aware of citizens who have created twitter accounts for the sole purpose of following #ARwx in severe weather. In seeing how well the public responded, we also established a hashtag for earthquake information, #AReq.

Currently a gap exists in Arkansas with the ability to push information to multiple sites without having someone physically push a button, or multiple buttons. Social media is currently housed in public affairs and while one of us is on-call at all times, the sites are not monitored 24/7. If alerts come out in the middle of the night, they do not get posted. To make up for this we have made it known that while we post some weather alerts, our social sites should not be anyone's single source of information for severe weather alerts. We direct people to the National Weather Service since they are the ones who issue the watches and warnings.

We are aware of the forthcoming Integrated Public Alert and Warning System (IPAWS) which is supposed to make it easier to issue warnings to citizens. Arkansas has elected to be a part of the pilot to test its abilities.

Recovery
Social media tools are useful in assisting in the recovery phase because they are able to bring the community together. Again, these sites enable us to talk with each other instead of to each other. Information about aid is able to be disbursed and then shared by anyone that wants to pass along the information. As individuals have questions they are able to direct them to us in a familiar format. We also post pictures of damaged areas to reinforce preparedness.

At this time the only privacy concerns I can see would be if someone was to discuss their assistance applications on a social site, asking ADEM for input. Assistance applications are not discussed through social sites. If a citizen was to initiate the conversation concerning their application the State's response would be to ensure the individual that they would be personally contacted regarding the status. Details are not to be discussed socially.

Barriers
The largest barrier was broken when our federal family began engaging in social sites. Before then, it was difficult for states and locals to say they were going to do something, or that it was acceptable to do something that the federal government had not yet adopted.

I believe that the federal government can work with social media companies to create a uniform analytics application for emergency managers to use. This would help emergency personnel see what messages were being received and which messages should need to be approached differently.

Conclusion
Thank you for the opportunity to provide testimony today and I look forward to any questions the Subcommittee members may have.

American Red Cross

Embargoed until Delivery
Wednesday, May 5, 2011
10:00 am (EDT)

For more information, contact:
Neal Denton, Govt Relations
202/303-4348

TESTIMONY OF SUZY DEFRANCIS
CHIEF PUBLIC AFFAIRS OFFICER
AMERICAN RED CROSS

Before the U.S. Senate Homeland Security & Governmental Affairs Committee
Subcommittee on Disaster Recovery & Intergovernmental Affairs

Understanding the Power of Social Media as a Communication Tool as We Prepare For
and Respond to Disasters

Good afternoon Mr. Chairman, Members and staff of the Subcommittee. This is a very timely gathering to address an extremely important subject, and we appreciate the opportunity to provide our perspective.

The recent deadly storms across much of the South and Midwest – as well as the earthquake and tsunami in Japan in March – underscore the urgency of working together with government and all our partners to be ready to respond whenever disaster strikes. Social media is playing an increasingly important role in helping people prepare for and respond to emergencies, and we look forward to sharing with you today our experiences with social media in recent disasters.

As you know, the American Red Cross responds to nearly 70,000 disasters each year in communities across the United States. You will find the Red Cross there to help people in need whether they are down the street, across the country or around the world. Our work is made possible by charitable contributions generously donated by the American public, and we strive to be excellent stewards of our donors' dollars.

American Red Cross Survey on Social Media in Emergencies – July, 2010

The power of social media as a communications tool during disasters became clear to us in the aftermath of the earthquake in Haiti last year. The American Red Cross began receiving tweets from people trapped under collapsed buildings. Haiti lacked a responsive 9-1-1 system and with cell service down in the early hours, people sought help however they could.

Like many other disaster-relief organizations and emergency responders, the American Red Cross didn't have a good way to handle those pleas. We had to go through messages manually and try to route them to the right places. It was a sign to us that disaster response was being changed almost overnight by new technology.

So we decided to convene an Emergency Social Data Summit in August of last year to discuss this issue with other emergency response and disaster relief agencies, as well as the social media entities who were part of this growing phenomenon.

To inform the debate, the American Red Cross conducted a survey of web users, which showed many would turn to social communities to seek help for themselves or others during emergencies. And even more importantly, they expected first responders to be listening.

The online survey, conducted in July 2010, asked 1,058 adults about how they would use social media sites in emergency situations. The survey found that among web users, social media sites are the fourth most popular source for emergency information, just behind television news, radio and online news sites. More web users say they get their emergency information from social media than from a NOAA weather radio, government website or emergency text message system. One in five social media users also report posting eyewitness accounts of emergency events to their accounts.

The survey found that they would also use social media to ask for help. Our survey revealed that if people needed help and couldn't reach 9-1-1, one in five would try to contact responders through a digital means such as e-mail, websites or social media. If web users knew of someone else who needed help, 44 percent would ask other people in their social network to contact authorities, 35 percent would post a request for help directly on a response agency's Facebook page and 28 percent would send a Twitter message to responders.

The Red Cross survey last summer also suggested that Americans have high expectations about how first responders should be answering their requests. For example, 69 percent said that emergency responders should be monitoring social media sites in order to quickly send help—and nearly half believe a response agency is probably already responding to any urgent request they might see.

And the survey respondents expected quick responses to online appeals for assistance—74 percent expected help to come less than an hour after their tweet or Facebook post.

Those were some eye-opening expectations. And we know that they don't match reality.

Another survey, taken just a month before, of members of DomPrep40, an advisory board of disaster response practitioners and leaders, found that 9 in 10 of the respondent groups were not staffed to monitor or respond to requests via social media platforms during major events.

We know that the first and best choice for anyone in an emergency situation is to call 9-1-1. However, as was recently reported in the *Washington Post*[1], 9-1-1 systems are slow to evolve in this digital age. When phone lines are down or the 9-1-1 system is overwhelmed, people will turn to social media.

Emergency Data Summit – August 12, 2010
The Emergency Social Data Summit was convened by the Red Cross on August 12, 2010 in Washington, DC.

---

[1] "Texting 911, Emergency Line Just Doesn't Get It." Sunday, April 24, 2011, *the Washington Post*. http://www.washingtonpost.com/local/texting-911-emergency-line-just-doesnt-get-it/2011/03/28/AF3VKnXE_story.html

DeFrancis Testimony for American Red Cross – May 5, 2011 page 2

More than 150 people attended the all-day Summit to talk about how best we can all engage social media to improve upon disaster preparedness and our collective disaster response. And while 150 were in the building, another 1,200 contributed virtually to the conference via Ustream and Twitter. It was quite a sight to see people live-blogging and tweeting in the same Red Cross Headquarters where people once rolled bandages during World War I.

This gathering marked the first time that government, nonprofit, technology, and citizen sectors came together to discuss the opportunities and challenges we face in integrating social data with disaster response. This hearing today will give these issues even more prominence, and we appreciate your leadership in these discussions.

A wide range of ideas and questions came out of the day-long conference, with seven key questions emerging:
- What can we do to prepare in advance of a crisis?
- Who should have custody of emergency social data? How should it be used?
- Can we codify a solution for routing this data to the proper places?
- What about the issues of accessibility to social media among people with disabilities?
- How do we avoid duplication of effort in responding to pleas for help?
- What is the best way to authenticate requests?
- How do we manage citizen expectations for response?

After the summit, we prepared a document entitled, "The Path Forward." This overview examined some of the issues, opportunities and challenges surrounding each of these questions. I have attached a copy of that document to this testimony.

The questions identified after the Emergency Social Data Summit will not be answered today and will probably not be answered tomorrow. Nevertheless, as your Subcommittee engages in this important conversation about social media in disaster response, they present a good basis for the discussion.

Today, for the purposes of this hearing, I'd like to focus on how the American Red Cross is exploring social tools to assist us in meeting the needs of those affected by disaster.

The American Red Cross and Social Media in a Disaster
For over 130 years, the American Red Cross has continued to operate in a constant cycle of responding to disasters and preparing for the next one. The tools we use to respond to disasters have evolved over the years – but perhaps the most exciting innovations are coming just now as we better understand the opportunities presented by advances in social technologies.

It may seem incongruous for an institution as old as ours to be embracing social media, but our experience teaches us that people in a crisis will communicate the same way they are used to communicating every day. Today, people are communicating with their family and friends on a daily basis through social media, so that is how the Red Cross must communicate. We currently have about 285,000 Facebook fans and 362,000 Twitter followers, and I am proud of the innovative work or team is doing to make social media a valuable part of our 21st century disaster response.

We use these tools to keep the public informed about relief efforts and to offer preparedness tips in real time. When a disaster occurs, we immediately acknowledge the situation by posting a status update to Facebook, a Tweet, a short video to YouTube, and a post to the Disaster Online Newsroom and our blog. We let our stakeholders know that we will update them with information about our relief efforts as they happen. While there's still much room for improvement, we have honed our standard operating procedures to provide nearly real-time information, action items, and tips.

We train Red Cross volunteers who deploy to disasters to use their smart phones and social technologies. These volunteers create new content from the field to better and more openly share the Red Cross relief efforts.

Mobile technologies and satellite communications are bringing everyone—humanitarian organizations, international institutions, volunteer technical communities, and the affected populations—ever closer together.

Using tools provided by social media partners such as Google Maps, the American Red Cross is collecting and compiling information that we never have been able to collect in the past. We are listening to those affected by disaster and we are sharing updates and information with partners and responders. We are building social media into our operational DNA.

Getting Help
The Red Cross uses these tools to empower our stakeholders to get help or give help.

First, getting help. As indicated in our survey, increasing numbers of people rely on their social community during crises. More often than not, victims of disasters can communicate via text messages, Twitter and Facebook in real time.

We have built a dynamic shelter map using Google maps to update our open shelter information every 30 minutes. We provide this information to the public through a public-facing portal and map on *www.redcross.org*. We also built an iPhone app so people on the move can access shelter information.

We are in the process of creating an official digital volunteer role that will help monitor, authenticate and route incoming disaster requests and information to other colleagues and partners. This kind of training allows remote employees and colleagues to assist in the disaster response efforts too. Colleagues using hash tags like #crisisdata, #redcross or something similar can collect, collate and respond to queries and concerns from their own homes.

Giving Help
Second, we use social media tools to empower people to give help. Our mobile fundraising efforts have made it easier than ever for donors to make donations with a text. We first saw the power of texting after the earthquake in Haiti when we raised more than $32 million dollars via text - $10 at a time. Forty-one percent of donors were under age 34 indicating a new generation was giving, perhaps for the first time in their lives.

We have partnered with Facebook Causes to allow for donations within Facebook, and we've worked with Twitter to make it easy for people to give there, too. We are transparent as possible, give our stakeholders digital tools, and they are easily able to help inspire their own networks to become part of our mission.

Preventing and Preparing for an Emergency

In Haiti, the Red Cross saw 4 million SMS text messages successfully delivered to approximately half a million Haitians as part of the cholera response. Messages covered the symptoms of cholera, treatment and simple steps to prevent it, people learned about preparedness measures, how to clean drainage around their homes to reduce the risk of flooding; and store reserves of water, food and medicine. The campaign also promoted the free Haitian Red Cross recorded information line, which received 400,000 calls.

Domestically, text messages and alert systems allow for citizens to receive aggregate information and news alerts from emergency response agencies and other media outlets. The public can be instantly informed about emergency situations, weather hazards and what actions should be taken to respond to that emergency. These alerts are pushed out further through social media. And citizen reports supplement this information and provide responders with additional situational awareness.

This expansion of warning systems is exemplified in many communities like in King County, Seattle where the Regional Public Information Network keeps the public informed about potential hazards and offers updates on emergency response. The network is also integrated with 9-1-1 and the local fire dispatch log.

Mr. Chairman, as you and your colleagues continue to explore the possibilities of social media, the answers to some of your questions will be found at the local level. We believe a local response is the most effective response because it all begins with individuals, families and communities.

Gaining Situational Awareness

When geodata is included in messages or when pictures are attached to a message – responders learn more about size, scope and necessary response for that location. This can prove to be a valuable tool in damage assessment following a disaster.

This operational data is important in how we approach reporting of sheltering activities. American Red Cross relief operations identify all locations and populations for all shelters and ensure this data is entered into the National Shelter System (NSS) database. The Red Cross NSS information is available through a downloadable application and contains location and capacity information for over 56,000 community facilities (schools, churches, etc.) that have been established as potential shelters across the country. The system records all shelter openings, closings and overnight populations on a daily basis, and is used to guide operational and planning decisions for multiple agencies at all levels. These comprehensive reporting practices and improved access to information allow us to more effectively identify and assess the needs of those affected by disasters as well as provide invaluable resources and information to the public seeking help.

Keeping Families Connected

In the first hours after a disaster strikes, an initial concern is to inform and connect family and friends. The American Red Cross is able to facilitate family communication through its Safe and Well website, found on www.RedCross.org. Here, individuals in affected areas may register their well-being using messages that can be seen by family and friends located outside the disaster area inquiring about their loved one's safety. Disaster victims also may update their Facebook and Twitter status through the Safe and Well website. Additionally, smart phone users may visit *www.redcross.org/safeandwell* and click on the "List Yourself as Safe and Well" or "Search for friends and family" link.

Correcting Misinformation

During the Summit, those gathered considered the need to authenticate and verify information. There is a balance between acting on information shared through social media outlets and ensuring what is transpired is accurate and correct. Because Red Cross colleagues are watching, tracking and engaging in social media during times of disaster, we are also quick to respond when misinformation is posted. We can often squelch misinformation quickly and decisively as we authenticate and verify information.

Building Resilience

FEMA Administrator Craig Fugate often speaks of his goal to have people see themselves as survivors and not victims of a disaster. "Social media can empower the public to be a part of the response, not victims to be taken care of." Social media enables neighbors to be a first responder to the immediate needs of their neighbors.

In catastrophic disasters we almost always see an abundance of hope from the unaffected – people want to tangibly help. We haven't previously been able to provide limitless valuable roles for these people, but with technology advances there are many opportunities to do just this, turning that abundance of care into more resilient communities, more effective disaster response, and more valuable partnerships.

Conclusion

Mr. Chairman and Members of the Subcommittee, thank you again for this opportunity to provide testimony today. We are excited to be working with this Subcommittee and your Congressional colleagues to explore the opportunities presented by engaging social media in our disaster preparedness and response.

The American Red Cross is committed to using all the tools of social media to improve our disaster response, but I would like to end with several thoughts:

If there is one thing that we've learned on this recent journey it is that we must continue to embrace change and remain open to new ideas and new platforms. Next year we may not be talking about Facebook or Twitter – but something entirely different. We need to be flexible and nimble.

And, if there's one thing that still must be addressed – it is a discussion of a potential increased role of Federal government. How can government better facilitate use of social media and new technologies to improve upon preparedness and disaster response?

The 2010 Summit participants were passionate about the need for a central, uniform system juxtaposed with *multiple* potential responsible parties including local responders, state agencies, nonprofits and, of course, the Federal government. Much discussion centered around the notion of porting data directly into the 911 system. The technical issues with texting are numerous and would require greater standardization by the entire wireless industry. While such a change could take years, some participants believe that intermediate steps could be taken to more easily share data between various agencies, local government and aid groups.

Finally, technology is a tool, not an end in itself. Our goal is to help alleviate human suffering and ensure that the country is as prepared as possible to respond to any disaster. We will use technology to do that, but it is not about the technology, it is about the people we serve.

Thank you again for your leadership. I am happy to address any questions you may have.

Testimony of Shona L. Brown, Senior Vice President, Google.org
Before the Senate Homeland Security Ad Hoc Subcommittee on Disaster Recovery and
Intergovernmental Affairs

Hearing on "Understanding the Power of Social Media as a Communication Tool in the Aftermath
of Disasters"
May 5, 2011

Chairman Pryor, Ranking Member Brown, and Members of the Committee.

Thank you for your focus on the important issue of crisis response and the central role that technology now plays in disaster relief and recovery. During the past year, tens of millions of people around the world have suffered through natural disasters such as earthquakes in Haiti, Japan, Chile, China, and New Zealand; floods in Pakistan and Australia; and forest fires in Israel. Our own citizens have faced crises, with tornadoes and floods causing terrible damage in recent weeks reminding us of the toll natural disasters have on human life. Our thoughts are with the communities that have just been hit by devastating tornadoes in Alabama and across the US.

As the Senior Vice President of Google.org, the philanthropic arm of Google, which includes the team that responds to natural disasters around the world, I have seen the increasing importance of Internet-based technologies in crisis response. Our team has used search and geographic-based tools to respond to over 20 crises in over 10 languages since Hurricane Katrina, and we have already responded to more crises in 2011 than we did all of last year. In the aftermath of the devastating tornadoes in Alabama last week, we supported the Red Cross by providing maps that locate nearby shelters, updated satellite imagery for first responders, and directed local users searching for "tornado" or "twister" to the maps through an enhanced search result.

Our work is modest in comparison to the work of emergency relief organizations and governments that are called to action, and our team does not claim to be expert in crisis response. We are computer scientists and developers, and Google.org is a newcomer to this space. We are still learning how we can help to respond to different types of crises. But our experiences have given us a unique vantage point on how powerful and robust a resource Internet-based technologies can be for both emergency responders and affected populations as they prepare for, respond to, and recover from a disaster. Here's why:

First, the Internet often remains available when other networks fail. The Internet was designed to be robust in the face of outages, and to automatically reroute through the path of least resistance. Its openness and interoperability continue to enable communication and access to information even when disasters render other means of communication unavailable. As a result, Internet-based emergency tools have proved to be quite reliable in disasters.

Time and time again, the Internet has served as a medium of communication when voice and text services are overburdened. Even when there is no power to boot up a computer, people are able to access the Internet through mobile devices to find emergency information or share their whereabouts.

Second, simple Internet technologies are often more effective than purpose-built technologies in emergencies. Google's products were not built as emergency-response tools, but we've found that they can be helpful in disasters. In emergency after emergency we see use of Google Search spike dramatically in affected areas, led by searches for information ranging from the status of loved ones to trustworthy information. Gmail and other Internet-based services like Google Maps are the tools of choice for many emergency responders who must be able to access email and documents anywhere in the world using whatever kind of operating system or connectivity they find. And Google Maps allows many response organizations to determine where to allocate resources. Organizations may, for example, use a familiar tool like Google Maps to make sure they set up their clinic next to a refugee center. This is because these technologies are simple, use common standards, and allow for open access.

Third, the Internet scales and allows different devices and applications to work together. The Internet Protocol has scalability at its core. This means that when demand increases to exceptional levels in an emergency, the Internet can handle it. Other communications networks are engineered with normal use patterns in mind and become overwhelmed quickly when these expectations are upset by disaster. The Internet Protocol also has openness in its DNA. An array of devices, using untold numbers of different applications, can all work together because of the way the Internet was built. These two strengths mean that the Internet allows tools created in response to one emergency to be rapidly iterated to fit the needs of a different emergency. For example, it took Google only 72 hours to create the Google Person Finder after the earthquake in Haiti. We managed to push the tool live just 90 minutes after the earthquake hit in Japan and made over 22 improvements to the tool during the crisis. This level of rapid iteration is something that is unique to Internet applications.

With these advantages of Internet-based technologies in mind, I would like to discuss the impact of three Google projects in recent relief efforts around the world: (1) Google Earth/Maps, (2) Person Finder, and (3) our efforts to make relevant news and information more readily available, such as through Crisis Response Landing Pages and enhanced search results.

Google Earth/Maps

In the emergency context, Google Earth, Google Maps, and Google MapMaker help organizations visualize assets geographically and make it easier for the affected population to find nearby emergency resources. Updated satellite imagery allows for quick damage assessments from thousands of miles away and can help relief organizations navigate disaster zones with, for example, crowdsourced information on available roads.

Last year's 7.0 magnitude earthquake in Haiti prompted us to scale existing tools to assist relief organizations. Organizations often use Google Earth and Maps to develop targeted relief plans, so we updated high resolution satellite imagery from our partner GeoEye within 24 hours of the earthquake and were the first to make such imagery available for public use. In addition, we collected 15-cm-resolution aerial imagery—much cleaner than a satellite can capture—of the affected region. This imagery has been used to conduct wide-scale damage assessments, plan response and recovery efforts such as clinic and hospital placements, and raise worldwide awareness of disasters.

A small Google team traveled to Haiti to better understand how our tools can be useful. We embedded with the 82nd Airborne in a refugee camp in what used to be the Petionville Golf Course. Soldiers from the 82nd used Google Maps to plan the routes they would take while patrolling the area. One of the officers explained to our team that they used Google Maps because "they use tools they're used to."

We found the same to be true after the terrible recent flooding in Pakistan. In the US, we tend to take complete maps for granted. Long before the flooding, two Pakistani web developers decided that available maps of their country were inadequate. So they decided to fix that situation with Google MapMaker, and along the way became some of the top volunteer mappers in the world. All their work played a major role in

VerDate Nov 24 2008   10 51 May 17, 2012   Jkt 067635   PO 00000   Frm 58   Fmt 6601   Sfmt 6601   P:\DOCS\67635.TXT   JOYCE

helping Pakistanis in the aftermath of the floods last August, when 20 percent of Pakistan was underwater. In response to the emergency, we shared our MapMaker base data with UNOSAT, which is the United Nations' mapping agency. This mapping information was helpful to emergency responders working in that terrible disaster.

These two examples show how Google's flexible, familiar, Internet-based mapping technologies can be quite powerful in a crisis. And more recently, in the wake of the tornadoes in the Southeast US, we requested satellite updates from partners and published a map layer with any useful data we could find about the tornadoes.

Many other organizations have taken advantage of the open Internet and the ability to crowdsource information in order to do incredible mapping work. Open Street Map, for example, has been credited with making the most complete map of Haiti's roads ever by getting the Haitian Diaspora to volunteer their knowledge. Ushahidi, another technology nonprofit, also allows for the creation of maps illustrating, for example, political violence in Kenya that people report through Twitter, email, or SMS.

Person Finder

Now I'll turn to Person Finder. Person Finder is an open-source web-based application that allows individuals to check and post on the status of relatives or friends affected by a disaster. Before Person Finder was developed, those seeking missing loved ones had to sift through multiple websites, posting the same inquiries over and over, hoping that the person they were seeking happened to register with one of these websites. In Haiti, for example, we noticed that there were 14 different missing persons databases. They were not integrated, all were running on different infrastructure, and all had a different amount of data that together represented all missing persons records.

To make this process more effective and efficient, while continuing to leverage the power of crowdsourced information, our team built Google Person Finder to act as a central database, pushing and pulling the feeds from all 14 databases, and allowing users to search across the information in all of the databases. Google Person Finder accepts information in a common machine-readable format called PFIF (People Finder Interchange Format), which was created by Hurricane Katrina volunteers in 2005. Our team worked around the clock to build and launch Person Finder in less than 72 hours during the early days of the crisis in Haiti. We have now made this resource available in more than 42 languages.

While we've used Person Finder for several disasters over the past year, the 9.0 magnitude earthquake and tsunami that struck the Tohoku region of Japan on March 11 led to its biggest use. People around the world struggled to connect with their loved ones as telecommunications services flickered. With phone and SMS networks overburdened by traffic, it was difficult to find out if loved ones were alive and well. But the Internet generally continued to function well, and Person Finder became a critical tool.

The product is purposefully simple, fast, and easy to use. More importantly, it is backed by an open programmatic interface, or API. This means that different sites can update missing persons lists automatically using the common format. Because of this, The New York Times, CNN, NPR, and a number of other websites quickly integrated Person Finder, increasing the reach and resulting in a more complete list of missing persons.

Today, Person Finder is a completely open source tool with a healthy discussion group and numerous external contributors. Person Finder helped manage more than 55,000 records of missing persons in Haiti, 75,000 records in Chile, and more than 600,000 records after the earthquake in Japan. We saw over 36 million pageviews in the first 48 hours after that earthquake. That number is likely overwhelming to most organizations and even government agencies, but we have the infrastructure to handle that volume.

3

Our own Senior Product Manager Kei Kawai lives in California and was trying to get in touch with his family back in Japan after the earthquake. He confirmed each person's safety, but could not make contact with his wife's grandfather, who lives in a town called Soma City that largely got washed out by the tsunami. After posting to Google Person Finder, Kei was relieved when news arrived through a post on Person Finder the next day that his wife's grandfather was safe.

Centralized Information Points

The third Google project I'd like to discuss relates to getting affected populations up-to-the-minute information as a crisis unfolds. As I mentioned earlier, we know from past experience that people turn to the Web for information during crises. Within a few hours of the Japan earthquake, we placed an alert on the Google homepage for Tsunami alerts in the Pacific and ran similar promotions across News, Maps, and other services. As a Tsunami warning was also issued for Hawaii, we saw a massive spike in search queries originating from Hawaii related to "tsunami."

With so many people searching online for critical information, we added an enhanced search result so that people could connect with emergency information as easily as possible. For example, someone in Japan who did a Google search for their town name plus the word "blackout" would have seen the scheduled blackout information above the typical search results. This information was not easily available before our work and we had to scrape numerous government websites and convert the data into machine readable formats. In the case of the recent tornadoes in the US, we enabled enhanced search results for Alabama and surrounding states with a link to the maps. The enhanced results appear when local users search for "tornado" or "twister."

Access to and use of Google search is generally widespread and many people turn to us in emergencies. As a result, we often create central crisis response sites where information such as emergency numbers, access to temporary shelters, news updates, maps, videos, user generated content, and donation opportunities are aggregated. Millions of people visit these landing pages which are created in a matter of hours and sometimes linked to on the country specific Google homepage. Those seeking information on an emergency generally fall into three categories. First, people directly affected who are looking for information such as power outages, temporary shelter, and how to respond. Second, people indirectly affected looking for family in the area or looking to share useful information. And third, aid organizations looking for imagery, to coordinate their response, and for logistical assistance. Our landing pages seek to assist each group. Furthermore, these pages allow people around the world to learn more and make donations. Our past landing pages have driven many millions of dollars of donations to relief organizations.

How Governments Can Support Technology Efforts in Crisis Response

Now that I've discussed how Google is approaching the use of technology in emergencies, I'd like to discuss one big way that governments and other organizations can support these and future efforts—by maintaining and even enhancing the openness and interoperability of the information available on the Internet.

An open and interoperable Internet allowed users to track the recent Australian floods on an interactive map because the map used the Keyhole Markup Language (KML), a machine readable and crawlable format used to describe geographic information. An open standard, namely the People Finder Interchange Format, or PFIF, also allows Person Finder to access and coordinate more than a dozen different databases, which gave those seeking family and friends in Japan access to more than 600,000 records.

But openness and interoperability do not characterize all parts of the Internet. The ability of the Internet to capitalize on its potential of assisting in crises depends on both companies and governments improving how they share information. Using divergent standards slows collaboration and response time. But speedy and open access, powering the ability of users to share and communicate information, accelerates relief efforts.

4

To pursue some of the projects I've described, Google had to gather emergency information from government websites in arcane formats and then translate them into open standards. Sometimes the information was spread across numerous websites. Other times, the licensing status of the data was not readily apparent. And even today, some important data is not even online at all, but is in someone's spreadsheet on their personal computer.

On the other hand, for example, the open KML standard, allows people to quickly create maps about shelter locations, escape routes, and emergency plans—and it is so easy to use that you don't have to be an expert developer to build a map. Governments and NGOs such as the Red Cross that maintain such lists could use KML, and if they inform us when they surface this information in advance of a disaster, we could feature it on our pages. It helps if this collaboration occurs in advance of a disaster, not in the middle of an emergency.

Similarly the PFIF allows organizations and users to easily upload information with a common format and to speak a simple common language so we can identify individuals in a consistent manner, making it simple for computers to automate the process of syncing multiple databases. Without this open platform and common standard, efforts to find missing persons become less coordinated and far more taxing on all parties. We ask organizations with missing persons databases to adopt the PFIF standard and encourage local governments and police to use PFIF as well. The troubling truth is that many organizations gathering missing persons information—as well as other critical data such as public health information—continue to do so on paper. The result is that we find boxes of unprocessed forms sitting in offices long after we have lost the chance to use them to help people. Wide adoption of PFIF can help.

And lastly, we recommend adoption of better alerting systems that leverage the Common Alerting Protocol (CAP) standard to quickly inform users of impending crises such as tsunamis and everyday alerts including transit delays. The Integrated Public Alert and Warning System operated by the Department of Homeland Security is a great first step. Agencies such as NOAA, for weather alerting, and USGS, for earthquake notifications, have done a great job being early adopters of CAP, but they require resources to improve the initial work they've done and allow for a truly robust Internet based warning system.

With better alerting systems, if they are implemented in an open and interoperable fashion, private actors such as Google could interact with government systems to display alerts tailored to geography, vulnerability, and situation. And we could do so in an open manner so any other Internet company or emergency organization could use or build on it.

Conclusion

I would like to conclude by thanking Chairman Pryor, Ranking Member Brown, the members of the Senate Committee on Homeland Security and other Members of Congress who have taken an interest in technology and crisis response. We will continue to work to help users instantly find the information they need when crises hit. We recommend the adoption of simple, open, and standard ways of publishing and disseminating information. And we look forward to working with you, government agencies, and emergency relief organizations. We play a modest role in comparison to the actors who work on emergency relief as their core mission, but we will continue to try and improve the use of Internet-based technologies for preparedness, response, and recovery, whether the emergency is a Pacific tsunami or tornadoes in the South.

VerDate Nov 24 2008   10 51 May 17, 2012   Jkt 067635   PO 00000   Frm 61   Fmt 6601   Sfmt 6601   P:\DOCS\67635.TXT   JOYCE

Testimony of Heather Blanchard, Co Founder of CrisisCommons before

the Ad Hoc Subcommittee on Disaster Recovery and Intergovernmental Affairs

Homeland Security and Governmental Affairs Committee

United States Senate

May 5, 2011

Good morning Chairman Pryor, Ranking Member Brown, and distinguished members of

the Subcommittee. My name is Heather Blanchard, and I am a co-founder of CrisisCommons, a

volunteer technology community that connects people and organizations who use open data and

technology to innovate crisis management and global development. Before this position, I spent

seven years at the U.S. Department of Homeland Security, including Deputy Director of the

Ready Campaign. On behalf of our community, it is a true honor to testify before you today.

When a crisis occurs, it isn't emergency responders who are first on the scene. It's everyday

people who use everyday resources like their mobile phone and social networks to share what

they know. This could be a road blocked by a tree after a storm or creating a map of where they

see wildfires. Today, there are many volunteers who leverage technology, like CrisisCommons,

that can direct technical capacity, harness open data and collaborative tools to help first

responders and communities make sense from the deluge of information that occurs in a crisis.

We believe that information at the right time and right place can help response authorities and

citizens make better decisions especially in a crisis.

Since the spring of 2009, CrisisCommons has been an open forum to explore how

information, including social media, can help in a crisis. Our community has supported

organizations and citizens in the response to the Haiti and Japan earthquakes, Tennessee floods, and last week's historic tornados which impacted the south east. Just to share an example, during the blizzard which paralyzed Chicago this year, our volunteers through CrisisCampChicago in collaboration with Humanity Road supported the Chicago Tribune Snow Map to assure that public requests for assistance were routed to 311 and other local authorities. One challenge we often see is that government agencies simplify the use of social media as a public affairs function when in fact, during a crisis, access to citizen-generated information is an operational necessity. As an example, this year during our support for the National Level Exercise the situational awareness workgroup that we participated in struggled to define how social media information would be coordinated from an operational perspective as there is not a resourced function which connects open data, including social media, and leverages potential surge capacity from communities like CrisisCommons. We would like to recommend to the committee that government create an operational liaison function which connects volunteer technology communities to our response systems at the Federal, State and local levels and be resourced for support during steady state and in crisis events. We recommend that current emergency management doctrine be revised to include the capability to harness technology volunteer expertise and collaborative systems.

Another challenge we have observed, is that in local Emergency Operations Centers the connection between social media information and operations is largely absent. We were shocked to find that some centers lacked high bandwidth Internet, technical skills or collaborative tools. We were also dismayed to find that many agencies have stringent security policies blocking their workforce from using social media tools for operational purposes. Without this capability emergency managers could be missing critical information in their operational picture. We recommend that emergency management infrastructure be fully modernized. We also recommend that policy and incident management doctrine be modified to allow emergency management personnel to engage outside of their own organizational networks to take advantage of social media tools and capabilities.

As you can see, emergency management is not prepared to utilize social media tools and data to augment their operations and inform their mission priorities. When there is a crisis, emergency management continuously find themselves overwhelmed with information. We recommend that resources be devoted towards helping emergency managers with data preparedness and filtering, increasing the level of digital literacy of the emergency management workforce and empowering their ability to connect with technology support.

In looking at the government's role in this ecosystem, the days of agencies passively sitting on the social media sidelines from behind the firewall are over. The time has come to evolve to a more open and participatory crisis management model. We believe that the Federal government has a leadership role to play but again, we feel that institutional support is needed to move us to the next level. To emphasize we recommend the following:

- Create an operational liaison function to coordinate with volunteer technology communities

- Revise policy and incident management doctrine to incorporate social media and other technology capabilities

- Invest in modernization of emergency management infrastructure and collaborative tools

- Support data preparedness and filtering, increasing the level of digital literacy of the emergency management workforce and empowering their ability to connect with technology support.

In spite of these challenges, we know of many emergency managers who are pushing the envelope everyday, sometimes at a professional risk, to apply social media tools and data in their work. We are supportive of enlightened leadership that Administrator Fugate displays everyday. He has opened the door to discussion and experimentation that we see today. However, individuals cannot change institutional challenges by example. Today we are asking for your help to support the needed enhancements that emergency management needs to fully utilize social media information and providing connectivity to communities who can support their efforts like CrisisCommons.

Thank you very much for the opportunity to testify before you today. I look forward to answering any questions you may have.

**Statement for the Record of Heather Blanchard, Co Founder of CrisisCommons
before the Ad Hoc Subcommittee on
Disaster Recovery and Intergovernmental Affairs**

**Homeland Security and Governmental Affairs Committee
United States Senate
May 19, 2011**

Good morning Chairman Pryor, Ranking Member Brown, and distinguished members of the Subcommittee. My name is Heather Blanchard, and I am a co-founder of CrisisCommons, a volunteer technology community that connects people and organizations who use open data and technology to innovate crisis management and global development. Before this position, I spent seven years at the U.S. Department of Homeland Security, including serving as Deputy Director of the Ready Campaign. On behalf of our community, it is a true honor to testify before you today.

When a crisis occurs, it isn't emergency responders who are first on the scene. It's everyday people who use everyday resources like their mobile phone and social networks to share what they know. This could be alerting authorities of a road blocked by a tree after a storm or creating a map of where they see wildfires. Today, there are many volunteers that can direct technical capacity and harness open data and collaborative technologies to help first responders and communities sift through and make sense from the deluge of information received during a crisis. We believe that information at the right time and right place can help response authorities and citizens make better decisions especially in a crisis.

Since the spring of 2009, CrisisCommons has been an open forum to explore how information, including social media, can help in a crisis. Our community has supported organizations and citizens in the response to the Haiti and Japan earthquakes, Tennessee floods, and last week's historic tornados which impacted the south east. For example, during the blizzard which paralyzed Chicago this year, our volunteers, through CrisisCamp Chicago and in collaboration with Humanity Road, supported the Chicago Tribune Snow Map (http://chicagosnow.crowdmap.com/) to assure that public requests for assistance were routed to 311 and other local authorities (see Figure 1). Just this month a collective of volunteer technology communities collaborated together to create Alabama Recovery Map (http://recoveryalabama.com/). Volunteers curated social media, developed data layers such as locations of Disaster Recovery Centers and local shelters to share trends of public needs and to provide a prototype example of support that can be provided to emergency operations centers to support local emergency response and recovery.

A "Whole of Community" Contribution

This Statement for Record reflects activities and observations of hundreds of volunteers and participants of open forum events, workgroups and communities. Initial findings provided in this Statement for the Record are based on engagement with emergency management practitioners and their perspectives as shared through the Social Media in Emergency Management Initiative, especially during observation and planning for exercises such as 2010 Golden Guardian and the 2011 National Level Exercise. Perspectives also have been taken from participants of the Missing Persons Community of Interest and from the global and open community of CrisisCommons.

At the end of this Statement of Record there is an Attachment A, which highlights contributions from the Missing Persons Community of interest such as the National Libraries of Medicine, CrisisCommons and Google as well as individual subject matter experts such as Tim Schwartz and Ka-Ping Yee who provided an overview of the People Finder Interchange Format (Missing Persons data standard) and observations from the Haiti response. In Attachment B we provide a compendium of comments submitted by CrisisCommons volunteers, affiliated organizations such as the Pacific Disaster Center, fellow volunteer technology communities such as Geeks Without Bounds and practitioners from urban areas such as Seattle and Los Angeles. CrisisCommons provides an open forum for contribution from volunteers and technology communities

Social Media is Just One Point In the Spectrum

Social media is just one point of a larger spectrum of information that can be turned into data to support response operations and even make our communities more resilient. From pinpointing the closest heart defibrillator with a mobile phone, to being able to tagging a picture to share with first responders, decentralized information can create a real time "participatory" sensory network which our country's emergency management system needs to have the capability and capacity to engage and connect. Social media is just the beginning, when information has a location, it can become points on a map or can visualize needs being requested from the public. Information at the right time and right place might be able to keep people out of harms way. Data when provided to decision-makers can help response authorities make better decisions on who needs help and where to expend precious resources.

Based on the experiences we have had at CrisisCommons working with emergency managers from around the world, see four fundamental challenges to government using social media and other technology, open data and technology surge support capacity:

- Government agencies simplify the use of social media (often blocked from use within the emergency management workforce due to "cybersecurity" concerns) to a public affairs function when in fact, during a crisis, access to citizen-generated information is an operational necessity.

- Within many Emergency Operations Centers (EOC) connection between social media and other public information is largely absent from operations and logistics.

- Today's emergency management policy and doctrine and after action reporting provides little, if any, support, guidance, training and resources for use of social media and other technologies (including geographic information systems (GIS), volunteer crisismapping, mobile and gaming), open data and surge support from volunteer technology communities.

- Little if any focus, training, resources are provided to emergency management practitioners at any level of government to support data preparedness and filtering, enhancement of the level of digital literacy within the emergency management workforce and empowering practitioners ability to connect with technology support (including social media), especially in times of crisis.

Time of Transformation

Never before has the need been so great for the public sector to show leadership in this area as emergency management is a vital function for our society. This month, McKinsey Global Institute[1] focused on the explosive use of data in a recently released a report titled, *Big Data: The next frontier for*

---

[1] Big data: The next frontier for innovation, competition, and productivity (May 2011). *McKinsey Global Institute Publications.* Retrieved on May 19, 2011, from http://www.mckinsey.com/mgi/publications/big_data/index.asp

H605-41331-79W7 with DISTILLER

innovation, competition, and productivity. The report stated, "Drawing on detailed analysis of five domains—health care, retailing, the public sector, manufacturing, and personal location data—the research identifies five broadly applicable ways to leverage big data:

- **Making big data more accessible in a timely manner**. In the public sector, making data more accessible across otherwise separated departments can sharply reduce search and processing time. In manufacturing, integrating data from R&D, engineering, and manufacturing units to enable concurrent engineering can cut time-to-market.

- **Using data and experimentation to expose variability and improve performance.** As they create and store more transactional data in digital form, organizations can collect more accurate and detailed performance data on everything from product inventories to personnel sick days.

- **Segmenting populations to customize actions**. Big data allow organizations to create ever-narrower segmentations and to tailor services precisely to meet customer needs. This approach is well-known in marketing and risk management, **but can be revolutionary in places like the public sector**.

- **Replacing and supporting human decision-making with automated algorithms**. Sophisticated analytics can substantially improve decision making, minimize risks, and unearth valuable insights that would otherwise remain hidden. Such analytics have applications from tax agencies to retailers.

- **Innovating new business models, products, and services**. Manufacturers are using data obtained from the use of products to improve the development of the next generation of products, and to create innovative after-sales service offerings. The emergence of real-time location data has created a new set of location-based mobile services from navigation to people tracking."

McKinsey points to the turning point where data can drive transformation and innovation. To echo this sentiment, earlier in 2010, The Economist[2] shared in its own perspective in their special report on managing information, *The data deluge: Businesses, governments and society are only starting to tap its vast potential.* Within the report, an article entitled, *Data, data everywhere: Information has gone from scarce to superabundant* shares how significant these changes are in the way society operates:

> *"We are at a different period because of so much information," says James Cortada of IBM, who has written a couple of dozen books on the history of information in society. Joe Hellerstein, a computer scientist at the University of California in Berkeley, calls it "the industrial revolution of data". The effect is being felt everywhere, from business to science, from government to the arts. Scientists and computer engineers have coined a new term for the phenomenon: "big data".*

Today, people are sharing information in ways like never before. "Big data" may be the future, but lifesaving data is critical today. How we can we all help to find the critical information in a crisis. Challenges abound when people who need assistance can't find resources which may even be closely

---

[2] Data, data everywhere. (2010, February 25). *The Economist* . Retrieved on May 19, 2011, from http://www.economist.com/node/15557443

available. The American Red Cross reported in their *Social Media in Disasters and Emergencies Survey*[3] that:

- Nearly 3 in 4 participate in at least one online community or network;
- 82% participate in social media at least once a week, with nearly half participating everyday or nearly everyday;
- One in six (16%) have used social media to get information about an emergency;

Perhaps one of the most significant findings found that during an emergency, nearly half of the survey respondents would use social media to let loved ones know they are safe and even more dramatically, three out of four would expect help to arrive within an hour, with 55% believing help would arrive in less than 30 minutes if they posted a request for help on a social media website.

The American Red Cross research tracks the reality of what CrisisCommons sees everyday. For example, during the blizzards of 2011 citizens turning to the Web when they needed help. Take the below entry of the Chicago Tribune Snowmap:

> *"I need to get my mother to Ingalls hospital for treatment. Even ambulance can't get through!!!!! Please come through 127th and Aberdeen in those residential buildings"*

Literally within blocks was a local police station which could have potentially been able assist. Today, there is often no formal connectivity between these community-based information systems and emergency management authorities.

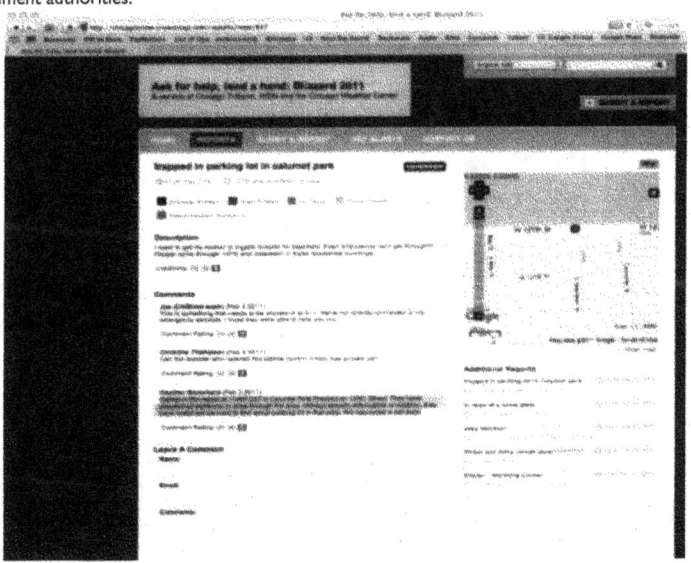

---

[3] Social Media in Disasters Survey. (2010, August 5) Retrieved on May 19, 2011 from http://www.redcross.org/www-files/Documents/pdf/other/SocialMediaSlideDeck.pdf

Figure 1. Chicago Tribune Snow Map, 2011

The amount of information is rising. In the February 2010 *The Economist issued a* special report on managing information where they forecast the skyrocking availability of global information created and the lacking ability to storage the data available. Today we are witnessing a transformation of not only how society communicates, including the use of social media, but its potential to link resources, to provide life saving information and its ability to help augment emergency management's understanding of the crisis event through more informed situational awareness and citizen reporting.

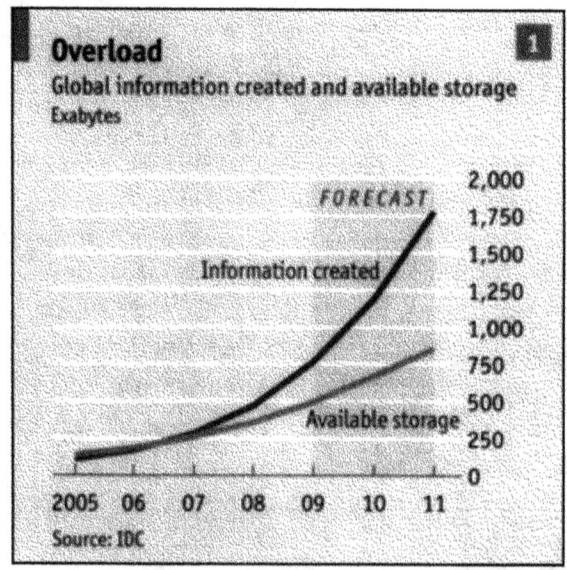

Figure 2. The Rise of "Big Data" from The Economist, February 25, 2010

Government Can Leverage Existing Capacity Today

Today, Federal government supports a myriad of siloed efforts which span across the Interagency that could be better coordinated to harness and prioritize efforts to ensure that capacity, resources and skill sets which already exist within the Federal government's domain can be effectively leveraged to support social media and other technology activities such as computation, modeling, visualization and aggregation. Potentially a new technology innovation and adoption coordination office within the Federal government could lead the strategic planning, incident coordination, technology outreach, training, education, research and development to raise the level of digital engagement and literacy of emergency management, ensure that emergency management priorities are incorporated into technology research and development innovation processes, lead partnership building and provide define problem sets for external collaborators, promote the use and release of open data. CrisisCommons recommends the exploration of the potential to leverage existing resources for greater capability, capacity and digital literacy:

- **Establish an Office for Technology Innovation and Adoption at FEMA to shepherd transformation needed within our nation's emergency management system at every level of government and affiliated partners.** This office could connect and leverage existing roles and resources and to lead the coordination of social media and other technologies (including GIS, crisismapping, gaming, mobile), incorporate the use of social media and other technologies (both within the response system and of society) into after action reporting, lead efforts to enhance the level of digital literacy and capabilities of emergency management, provide recommendations for the modernization of the emergency operations center model, prioritize research and development investment of existing Federal research and development funding, build sustainable public-private partnerships to leverage open data and volunteer technology communities, develop incident management role in accordance with the National Response Framework and the National Incident Management System, liaison to innovators and support rapid response community-based research and development.

- **Establish of an Interagency Crisis Technology Lab to create synergies within the Interagency.** This open innovation space could be an open forum which by design could seek to provide a unique collaboration and operations for the Federal Interagency to connect with emerging technologies, for State and local first responders and emergency management agencies to prototype new ideas and bring needs from the field and access tools and resources for organizations, including volunteer technology communities, for experimentation and crisis response with possibilities of branching to related areas such as public health and global development. This lab leverage the expertise from across the entire emergency management practitioner community while working alongside new collaborators such as technology volunteers, sociologists and engineers. Ultimately the lab, especially if centered within one of our nation's technology innovation corridors, could go a long way to seed transformational leadership across emergency management including technical skill development to support open data and free and open source tools and can act as a hub to coordinate technology requirements, coordination and potential field deployment during domestic and international crisis events.

Listening To Innovators Within Emergency Management Community

Through the emergence of social media technology over the past decade, individuals have experienced a fundamental shift in how they interact with the world, where they interact with it, and the speed at which interaction takes place. Recent crisis events have demonstrated the transformational impact of this technology with respect to emergency management and disaster response. What this promise looks like was the topic of discussion at the Social Media in Emergency Management (SMEM) 2011 Camp, an event hosted by the National Emergency Management Association Mid-Year Conference and the SMEM Initiative, a global emergency management practitioner community, in collaboration with CrisisCommons. CNA, a non-profit research center, provided a volunteer research team to support data collection and white paper development.

In the past two years, much has been made by individuals in the response community of the effect of new technologies—including social media—on international disaster response efforts; receiving somewhat less attention has been the effect of these technologies on domestic initiatives. On March 24, 2011, over 150 individuals within the domestic response community and with various levels of technology expertise convened for the first time for a day of learning and discussion on the value of social media and

H605-41331-79W7 with DISTILLER

emergent technologies, best practices, and challenges relevant to the adoption and use of technology in emergency response. Attendees represented a broad cross-section of the emergency response community and included representatives from FEMA (Administrator Fugate and Deputy Administrator Serino), the Red Cross, Twitter, state and local emergency management agencies, Canadian emergency management, the private sector, and various volunteer technology communities (VTCs). Topics for the breakout sessions were "crowdsourced," meaning that the participants themselves created and led the sessions based on their own interests in information sharing. During SMEM Camp, participants created the following sessions: Policy, Getting Started (Social Media 101), Community Building, Situational Awareness, and "Running your Shop."

One of the primary objectives of the conference was to capture discussion from the event and develop a white paper to highlight best practices, challenges, future engagement, and training opportunities. The white paper is scheduled for release to coincide with the June 2011 Urban Areas Security Initiative Conference in San Francisco, CA. Below is a discussion of the initial findings.

Insights Into What Is Needed

Discussions revealed that while there has been a great deal of progress in the use and integration of social media and related technologies in emergency response, there still remains a conceptual aspiration as to how these technologies can be used to improve response in both crises and steady-state situations. Currently, these technologies are predominantly used by Public Information Officers (PIOs) to provide awareness externally by disseminating information to the public, and internally by monitoring open-source information streams. However, participants expressed a desire to see these technologies used consistently across all spectra of the response apparatus, particularly operations, to leverage open data and the participatory community. The gap between the current state and the desired state of practice persists because of legitimate concerns and challenges that emergency managers (EMs) face in fostering adoption and creating internal and external buy-in. Participants also observed that many of the challenges are interrelated and that improvements or solutions in one area can set the stage for progress in other areas.

The following issues particularly resonated among camp participants:

- **Need for Resources:** To make full use of new technologies in an effective manner requires an investment and commitment of resources to that end. This commitment is currently not found across the majority of response agencies. Where advances have occurred they have largely been made by individual champions of these technologies who see value and have pushed for their use. The lack of institutional support limits use to convenience, inherently stunting its development as a tool for emergency management. In lieu of funding for increased personnel and training, EMs who use these technologies have had to assume an inordinate workload or rely on Volunteer Technology Communities (VTC) that have demonstrated the ability to curate, filter, and synthesize critical response information.

- **Need for Policy and Guidance:** The lack of clearly defined legal and policy guidance around privacy, liability, reliability of information, and appropriate use has made many EMs hesitant to use these new technologies. Without a defined role for use of these technologies within the federal emergency response framework, their use has been limited primarily to the PIO role. Development of policies for use across all response components will need to be supported with guidance and best practices at the federal level, which will help remove hesitancy, provide templates for implementation, and increase adoption at the state and local levels. Additionally, as VTCs are increasingly used to help augment

VerDate Nov 24 2008   10 51 May 17, 2012   Jkt 067635   PO 00000   Frm 72   Fmt 6601   Sfmt 6601   P:\DOCS\67635.TXT   JOYCE

response personnel, volunteer liability and integration within the response structure will need to be addressed.

- **Need for Engagement and Community Building:** Establishing a sustained dialogue between citizens and responders through new technologies will create value around their use. Not only is awareness created on both ends, but trust between the participating actors can be developed and leveraged during response. Community building before a crisis can both leverage the community as a force multiplier and help to manage public expectations around the use of new technologies during response, which EMs cited as a concern. Support for the development of and EM participation in continued learning opportunities, such as the SMEM 2011 Camp described above, will help to disseminate best practices and to develop a common understanding of how the response community can leverage these technologies for sustained constituent engagement.

- **Need To Demonstrate Value and Reliability to Others:** Several individuals who attended the camp walked in as skeptics but left ready to be champions for technology adoption within their organizations. An exchange of experiences helped sway these individuals; however, it still remains difficult to demonstrate value beyond anecdotal evidence. A lack of measurement with respect to impact and reliability of these tools in real-world response events leave many unaware or unconvinced of their value. Initiatives that will allow for increased data collection and assessment of technology and its use in response will be critical in creating buy-in at all levels of response.

Changing the Discourse to Focus on Data and the User-Defined Operational Picture

One challenge we often see is that government agencies characterize the use of social media as a public affairs function when in fact, during a crisis, access to citizen-generated information is an operational necessity. As an example, this year during the 2011 National Level Exercise, the situational awareness workgroup participants struggled to define how social media information could be coordinated from an operational perspective. Currently there is not a resourced function that connects the response community to open data, including social media, and leverages the potential surge capacity from volunteer technology communities like CrisisCommons.

Through the course of discussions, CrisisCommons reached to the Social Media in Emergency Management Initiative partnerships to provide feedback to FEMA's Situational Awareness Workgroup. The SMEM participants developed five opportunities for improvement:

- **Re-scope situational assessment.** The workgroup found that the concept of the "Common Operating Picture" needs to be redefined to include distributed open data and its consumption versus data in "one centralized place" and preferential selection of specific platforms. The reality is that an incident commander in the field has different data needs than the Director of the National Response Coordination Center. This is also true at the State level where State operations, logistics and planning sections need to make sense of and visualize data from a their different perspective but access common datasets. In addition to emergency management authorities, stakeholders and affiliated response partners (including volunteer technology communities) should have access and knowledge of how to incorporate data into their own, user-defined operational picture.

- **Create a data coordination role:** The workgroup found the need to unite existing technology (including GIS) capabilities and shore the ability for the National Response Coordination Center needs to be able to leverage existing technology and human capital resources which the Federal government can bring to bear to support State and local response efforts as requested by State Governors as well as to support international humanitarian response as requested by USAID. Within an emergency operations center the technology cluster team with representation from all Emergency Support Functions (ESF) function areas could work together to provide resources to support the entire emergency response. Since data feeds into decision-makers, the reporting structure of the Technology Cluster should have a Special Advisor (leadership level) to the leadership of the incident, replicated at all levels of government: local, State, Tribal, and Federal. This entity could have external collaboration functions with the private sector and with volunteer technology communities. To support this role within the overarching emergency response system, the National Incident Management System (NIMS), National Preparedness Framework, National Response Framework and National Disaster Recovery Framework could to be updated to incorporate the use of data and this liaison process through the emergency management cycle.

- *Focus on data, especially open data, not platforms.* The workgroup found that often conversations get mired in which platform to use rather than "What kind of data can we use and from what source?" or whether or not existing data in those systems (and the systems themselves) can talk to each other and be shared to affiliated partners and the public through data feeds. The role of government should be to provide as many data feeds to the public, any operational requirements needed by the operational elements and contextual support if necessary.

- *Enhance data planning and interoperability.* The workgroup found that there was a need for a data interoperability planning matrix. This matrix could identify the critical data sets and shows the flow/exchange of data from the data creators (sources) to the data users. This matrix could be the foundation of a planning document that could include all data as needed by a technology cluster with a focus on fostering the expedited use of common data sets between responding organizations. The matrix could be used to identify data sources, essential sources of information, format, location, access control, security and other meta-data Other data planning should include defining what data is required to emergency management in the planning and mitigation phase and making it is easily searchable, accessible, malleable, and available (shareable).

- *Focus on user defined/dynamic operational picture.* The workgroup found that information in a dynamic operational picture should be scalable and available at each level: local, state, national, NGO, etc. Often interoperability is thought to be about the movement of data from one system to another, whereas interoperability also should include access to the right data. Moving data increases complexity and resources as well as liability and privacy requirements to store and maintain the data. In the end, the effort to provide data access could allow each operational unit to query datasets, and only move and manage what is critical and/or required. Each unit can determine what information they need for their operational picture, creating dynamic user-based operational pictures which can answer critical questions.

Modernize Emergency Management's Operations Center

Another challenge we observed is that within our nation's Emergency Operations Centers (EOC), the vital connection between social media information and operations is largely absent. We were shocked to find that some centers even lacked high bandwidth Internet and other centers did not have the "people skills" or the latest technology tools to do their jobs. In smaller communities, the EOC, if present at all, is connected to an already busy 911 Center. We were also dismayed to find that many agencies have stringent security policies blocking their workforce from using social media tools for operational purposes. Without this capability emergency managers could be missing critical information in their operational picture.

VerDate Nov 24 2008   10 51 May 17, 2012   Jkt 067635   PO 00000   Frm 74   Fmt 6601   Sfmt 6601   P:\DOCS\67635.TXT   JOYCE

- CrisisCommons recommends that **emergency management infrastructure be fully modernized** at the Federal, State and local levels and be fully resourced **to support data coordination needs** during steady state and in crisis events.

- CrisisCommons recommends that **emergency management doctrine and policy be revised** to allow emergency management personnel to engage outside of their own organizational networks to take advantage of social media tools and capabilities.

Today, emergency management may not be adequately equipped to utilize social media tools, technologies and data to augment their operations and inform their mission priorities. When there is a crisis, emergency management continuously find themselves overwhelmed with information.

- CrisisCommons recommends that **resources be devoted towards helping emergency management practitioners** with data preparedness and filtering, increasing the level of digital literacy of the emergency management workforce and empowering their ability to connect with technology support.

Government's Role in Social Media and Emergency Management

In looking at the government's role in this ecosystem, the days of agencies passively sitting on the social media sidelines are over. The time has come to evolve to a more open and participatory crisis management model. We believe that the Federal government has a leadership role to play but again, we feel that institutional support is needed to move us to the next level. To emphasize we recommend the following:

Prioritize, connect and leverage existing Federal resources to support transformation and innovation

Similar to the U.S. Department of Defense's "J9" Joint Concept Development and Experimentation Directorate which was established to help the military transform itself to enable enhanced collaboration with non-military stakeholders and the federal interagency. FEMA could learn from this established capacity and develop a new FEMA Office of Technology Innovation and Adoption whose mission is to leverage social media and other technologies (such as GIS, volunteer crisismapping, gaming and mobile); liaison with innovators and volunteer technology communities, harness existing resources available today within the Federal family that can be brought to bear to support State, Tribal and Local emergency management and community resiliency; and raise the level of digital literacy of the emergency management practice area (including Disaster Assistance Employees).

This office could coordinate training and social media technology development, implementation, and use through all aspects of the emergency management cycle and could lead the Federal government's crisis response social media function during domestic and, as requested by USAID, international humanitarian response efforts.

To ensure resources and leadership required, this office could be a direct report to the FEMA Administrator and could be charged with coordination for the following tasks:

- Ensure the full use of the federal government skills and resources are brought to bare during all phases of the disaster continuum;

H605-41331-79W7 with DISTILLER

- Improve the level of digital literacy and use of technology through the emergency management practice area, including the VOAD and Faith-Based and Community organizations;
- Provide policy requirements and technical assistance for FEMA Grant Guidance to ensure the ability for State and local emergency management to fully utilize federal funding and resources to support operational technology needs, emergency operations center modernization, human capital investment, community-based technology innovation programs, developer development programs, community data coordination and collection efforts.
- Provide policy requirements and development assistance to create, develop or revise incident management doctrine, including all frameworks - especially the National Response Framework and the National Incident Management System.
- Coordinate incident response roles and responsibilities for the FEMA Administrator. This office could lead coordination across all Emergency Support Functions and support leadership, operations and external affairs. This incident response role must straddle all ESFs. This role should be reflected at all levels of government.
- Provide strategic coordination, partnership development and planning guidance to ensure that government resources at all levels of government can be maximized. Work with established partnerships to connect coordination hubs for government agencies and external partners, such as the private sector, academia, volunteer technology communities, and other organizations can coordinate technology and open data needs, incident management roles, best practices and lessons learned.
- Conduct technology after action reports for the federal family on the use of technology by response agencies and affiliated partners as well as with civil society. This office could provide and guide operational implementation of recommendations.
- Lead the revision and coordination efforts of emergency management policy and incident management responsibilities as it relates to the use of technology, including technology volunteers and private sector assets across the Federal family.
- Lead the identification, requirements and appropriate release of critical federal data assets, including aerial and satellite imagery, needed to support all aspects of emergency management . As appropriate, provide access to data and imagery to support the activities of the volunteer technology communities, including aerial and satellite imagery.
- Lead innovation and collaboration across the federal family and building partnerships with communities, including volunteer technology communities, to enhance our nation's ability to respond to crisis through the development and management of a Interagency Crisis Technology (ICT) Innovation Lab and Technology Operations Center; and
- Support data preparedness and filtering through training and education of the FEMA and other Interagency support functions, provide`ding guidance and policies that encourage data feed sharing;
- Identify pre-scripted mission assignments of existing Federal assets such as NGA aerial and satellite imagery, Federal Labs for modeling and computation, and DHS Centers of Excellence for social behavior and visualization.
- Survey, benchmark and provide programs and tools, data and training to increase the level of digital literacy of the emergency management workforce, including Disaster Assistance Employees, and empowering their ability to connect with technology support.
- Lead FEMA's external technology planning efforts with other technology response efforts such as the National Cyber Incident Response Plan and support leadership liaison roles to existing advisory councils such as the National Telecommunications Advisory Council, National Infrastructure Assurance Council, data privacy committees and other interagency workgroups which support functionality.

- Create an Administrator Technology Innovation Fellow Program at every skill level to provide the ability for established emergency management practitioners and technology professionals to work together on common goals to support Innovation objectives both in Washington and Silicon Valley.
- Leverage the FEMA Loaned Executive Program to bring highly skilled professionals from the technology and telecommunications sectors and other areas to advise FEMA on operational opportunities to encourage modernization, use of open data and skill enhancement of the emergency management practice area.
- Establish and coordinate the development of a public-private sector Technology Advisory Committee under the FEMA National Advisory Council which could include representation from the private sector (especially social media companies), academia, NGOs, nonprofits, VOADs and volunteer technology communities.

Connect and *leverage existing resources to create a common innovation and research space for collaboration, experimentation, operational response and education*

To ensure that FEMA can tap resources within the private sector and leading research institutions, FEMA should establish the Interagency Crisis Technology (ICT) Innovation Lab which reports to the Office of Technology Innovation. This open lab will be the first of its kind to be specifically designed to exist outside of government systems, and be connected to our nation's leading technology innovation hubs outside of Washington DC, whose mission is to harness the existing capacity and capability of existing Federal resources, such as visualization, computation, analysis, imagery coordination and other assets which the Federal family can deploy to support a domestic or international humanitarian response. This center, lead by FEMA with founding partners from USAID, USGS, NGA, NOAA and NASA, could have an interagency representation to ensure that FEMA and USAID can draw upon all agencies who could have a role, resource or capability (both financial, technical and skills) to support State, local and when requested by USAID, international assistance.

This ICT Innovation Lab could house a U.S. Technology Operations Center where the Interagency, the private sector, academia, NGOs, volunteer technology communities and other affiliated response communities can coordinate a unified technology support response. This ensures the ability to create coordinated and shared requirements from FEMA to Interagency Partners and provide connectivity to the Technology and Telecommunications sectors to maximize the involvement and coordination with the external partners including the private sector and volunteer technology communities.

The ICT Innovation Lab could support open source development and coordinate an Emergency Management developer community to assist in the training, development, licensing and use of open source software for public use. FEMA and USAID should require within its funding mechanisms that all research and code development under the ICT Innovation Lab release findings, code and data through online, collaborative sharing tools and require all data collection, products and their derivatives be licensed under Creative Commons or the appropriate open source software licensing to ensure the greatest amount of sharing and use by the public.

The ICT Innovation Lab could encourage the curation of team-based multi-disciplinary rapid research and establishment of long-term continuous improvement teams surrounding the use of technology by civil society and response authorities to establish continuous improvement research investment, especially community-based rapid response research. This could allow non-traditional knowledge curation through activities such as experiential learning, coding and gaming to supplement academic level findings based on real-time learnings. In addition, these findings could drive research investment priorities based on lessons learned from past events to ensure that federal research dollars through such agencies as National Academies of Science, Corporation for Public Service, Federal Labs, DHS and DoD Centers of Excellence and other organizations streamline research goals and objectives towards today's pressing crisis technology challenges.

We Need To Support Transformation and Innovation Today

In closing, despite today's current challenges, we know of many emergency managers who are pushing the envelope everyday, sometimes at a professional risk, to apply social media tools and data in their work. We are supportive of enlightened leadership that the Administrator Fugate displays everyday. He has opened the door to discussion and experimentation that we see today. However, individuals cannot change institutional challenges by example. Today we are asking for your help to support the needed enhancements that emergency management needs to fully utilize social media information and to provide connectivity to communities who can support their efforts like CrisisCommons.

VerDate Nov 24 2008   10 51 May 17, 2012   Jkt 067635   PO 00000   Frm 78   Fmt 6601   Sfmt 6601   P:\DOCS\67635.TXT   JOYCE

Attachment A - People Finder Interchange Format (PFIF)

Overview

People Finder Interchange Format (PFIF) is an open data standard for information about missing or displaced people. It was designed to enable information sharing among governments, relief organizations, and other survivor registries in order to help people find and contact their family and friends after a disaster.

The motivations for creating the PFIF standard dates back to 2001. Within three days of the attacks of September 11, 2001, people were using over 25 different online forums and survivor registries to report and check on their family and friends. One of the first and largest of these was the survivor registry at safe.millennium.berkeley.edu, which was created by graduate students Ka-Ping Yee and Miriam Walker and hosted on the Millennium computer cluster at UC Berkeley. To reduce the confusion caused by the proliferation of different websites, the Berkeley survivor registry began collecting data from several of the other major sites and aggregating this data in a single searchable database. Because the information was formatted differently from site to site, each site required manual effort and custom programming to download and incorporate its data.

After Hurricane Katrina displaced hundreds of thousands of people in 2005, online survivor registries again appeared on many different websites. A large volunteer effort called the Katrina PeopleFinder Project worked to gather and manually re-enter this information into a single searchable database provided by Salesforce.com. An organizer of the project, David Geilhufe, put out a call for technical help to create a data standard that would enable survivor registries to aggregate and share information with each other in an automated fashion. Working with Katrina volunteers Kieran Lal and Jonathan Plax and the CiviCRM team, Yee drafted the first specification for People Finder Interchange Format (PFIF), which was released on September 4, 2005. The Salesforce.com database added support for PFIF; Yahoo! and Google also launched searchable databases of Katrina survivors that exchanged information using PFIF.

PFIF In Action: Haiti Earthquake Response

Shortly after the January 12, 2010 earthquake in Haiti, in a similar fashion to the September 11 and Katrina events, a multitude of missing persons databases appeared, including haitianquake.com as well as sites created by news organizations, non-profits, aid groups, and individual technology volunteers. Within several informal networks, people began to recognize the need for a common system of information on missing persons.

On January 15, 2010, Google launched Google Person Finder, an open source, web-based application that allows individuals to check and post on the status of relatives or friends affected by a disaster. Ka-Ping Yee, one of the originators of PFIF, also led the engineering effort to build Google Person Finder, which used PFIF to allow press agencies, non-governmental organizations, and others contribute to its database and receive updates. In addition, websites could choose to embed Google Person Finder as a gadget on their own pages. In the coming days, CNN, the New York Times, and other sites began to exchange their missing persons data with Google Person Finder.

Julie Moos described the situation in a blog post at Poynter.org on January 17, 2010:

"While some news organizations were already interested in working with Google to share information, a formal call for their participation in the people finder project came Saturday from Christopher Csikszentmihalyi, director of the MIT Center for Future Civic Media. It circulated by e-mail and was published on David Pogue's New York Times blog and, in part, on Wired's web site."

In the call to news organizations, Csikszentmihalyi acknowledged that "many newspapers have put precious resources into developing a people-finder system." However, he explained, "This excellent idea has been undermined by its success: Within 24 hours it became clear that there were too many places where people were putting information, and each site is a silo."

"Sharing common data and making it all accessible is key, because if Jean Q. Publique enters a name of a missing loved one on one site, and another person says they have found that loved one on a different site, they will not connect." Csikszentmihalyi told me by e-mail.

Others were thinking of a single, centralized site as well, including designer Tim Schwartz, who created Haitianquake.com, a registry for tracking missing persons.

"I realized immediately that in our Web 2.0 environment, with tons of social networking sites, that missing people information was going to go everywhere on the Internet, and it would be very hard to actually find people and get back to their loved ones if everything was scattered," Schwartz said by e-mail. *"So, my initial goal was to create a unified database that would be the one repository for missing people data, and other online applications could connect to it."*

"That first night we had a database of 6,000+ entries where people could post images and leave updates on people in the database. By the next afternoon I had coordinated efforts with the development community and Google had just started to move on ideas about family reunification," he continued. *"We coordinated our efforts with them and by Friday morning Google had the beginning of their application out with an embeddable widget to take in data."*

Over the weekend, the 22,000 entries collected at Haitianquake.com were moved to Google's database, which Schwartz said was up to 30,000 records "and growing" as of early Sunday evening.

Google took on the role of main PFIF repository that Salesforce.com had played during the Hurricane Katrina response effort. PFIF 1.1, the version of PFIF used for the Katrina effort, had made several US-specific assumptions, so PFIF needed to be extended for the Haiti relief effort. Released on January 26, 2010, PFIF 1.2 added fields for the person's home country and international postal code, as well as fields for sex, age, date of birth, status, and links between duplicate records for the same person.

By design, all data entered into Google Person Finder is available to the public. The data resides on Google servers and is not verified for accuracy. Instead, Google Person Finder depends on individual users to update and remove outdated records. More information on how the data is used is available in the Google Person Finder FAQ.

Google was well positioned to launch a missing persons database due to 1) their ability to handle a very high volume of users and web traffic during crisis events, and 2) the perception of Google as a trusted partner by government, relief, and news organizations. The ease of embedding the Google Person Finder gadget enabled other organizations to use and promote the tool on their own sites as well. Later, Google leveraged its internal teams and process to translate the product into more than 40 languages, making it accessible to a broader audience of potential users.

After Haiti

The effort in Haiti was duplicated following the Chile Earthquake. A Google Person Finder instance was quickly established to help locate missing people. Over 78,000 records were entered into the Chile Person Finder instance. In the first 24 hours, the site was viewed over 2.5 million times. The Chile instance was supported in part by an all-volunteer technology community, Digitalas Por Chile (creators of ChileAyuda.com) who hosted CrisisCamp Santiago at the University of Chile on February 27, 2010 in collaboration with the World Bank. Volunteers worked to input missing persons' names into Google Person Finder.

With respect to retention of PFIF data, note that the US National Library of Medicine captures its own copy, and its retention policy and web sites are also evolving. As of this writing the Haiti data has been left up in searchable form at the original site (https://hepl.nlm.nih.gov). The National Library of Medicine has a newer multi-event "People Locator" site (https://pl.nlm.nih.gov) that has used PFIF to import post-Haiti reports, such as those from the Christchurch, New Zealand earthquake and the Tohoku disaster.

Since the Haiti and Chile responses, a full-time Crisis Response team has been formed within Google.org, the philanthropic division of Google. On November 15, 2010, Google.org posted an invitation to the developer community to help improve Google Person Finder and the PFIF data format. The open source code for Google Person Finder, a list of open issues and feature requests, and a Developer Guide are available at the project site on Google Code. Google also announced that it was closing the Google Person Finder instances for Haiti, Chile, China, and Pakistan, and stated:

> *"… we intend for each instance of Google Person Finder to be running for a limited time. Once an instance has served its purpose, we will archive the PFIF records in a secure location for historical preservation for one year while we work to identify a permanent owner for these records. Assuming a long-term owner cannot be found, we will delete the records after one calendar year."*

Developers at Google and elsewhere wanted a clearer solution for data privacy and deletion that could be added to the PFIF standard. PFIF 1.3, released in March 2011, addressed these concerns by adding an expiry date field to each Person record and setting out requirements for repositories to delete their data. The expiry date field allows users to specify how long they want a record to persist. Google changed its one-year data retention policy to follow these requirements, and Person Finder now defaults to expiring records after 60 days. PFIF 1.3 also moved away from the US-specific assumption of a first and last name by adding a single field for a person's full name.

At the conference for the International community on information systems for crisis response and management (ISCRAM 2011), representatives and developers from the Sahana Software Foundation, Google, the American Red Cross, and the National Library of Medicine convened a workshop to test, evaluate, and improve the ability of their missing person systems to interoperate with each other using PFIF.

Observations

Since January 2010, CrisisCommons has collected observations from these processes through the Missing Persons Community of Interest. Today there is an opportunity to create ongoing dialogue and continuous improvement processes on a domestic and international level. A few observations of the community included:

- During every crisis there will be new, more distributed and sophisticated data systems collecting and distributing missing persons information. Person Finder provided a direction for these efforts which allowed for replication of the missing persons widget but consolidated the data from potentially hundreds of systems to a small handful, with major media outlets in support of Person Finder.

- In official crisis response systems (i.e. International Committee of the Red Cross Family Links system or Red Cross Safe and Well) data is required to have high level of security and privacy governance. Information collected in Family Links comes from the ground.

- Official crisis response systems have resource challenges to modernize data systems, challenges in scale and providing technical surge support (from vendors or internal volunteers) during the crisis.

- Google has provided an open platform where missing persons information can be exchanged. Technology volunteers can place information about people into this system and people who are looking for loved ones can search the system for information.

- By providing an API, Google is allowing other organizations, especially response organizations whose role it is to collect and process missing person's information, to push and pull data from its system.

- Person Finder has data that are unverified. Official crisis response systems are reluctant to use unverified data or co-mingle that data with official missing person's data.

- Currently Google.org listens to the public and gauges the need for an instance. It has been discussed by Google.org and those within the volunteer technology community have discussed if there needs to be a governance body or set of processes in order to trigger an instance of Person Finder in the future.

The year 2010 saw an unprecedented use of the Person Finder application after natural disasters. Each launch, presented an opportunity to share lessons learned from users of Person Finder, official response systems such as ICRC Family Links, and unaffiliated volunteers. academia, such as the University of California, presented new technical methods including the need to improve the search capability of Person Finder tool provided by Google.

In October 2010, Tim Schwartz, a technology volunteer and CrisisCommons as a result of the initial conversations of the CrisisCamp After Action Report documenting the role of technology volunteers who supported Missing Persons data management began to led the development of a long term open membership community of interest which seeks to support the ongoing technical and policy development which can be improved after input and feedback from each crisis as well as the leveraging innovative development which can occur through hackathons and other open forum collaboration events. The Missing Persons Community of Interest provides an open forum for continued opportunity to broaden the discourse surrounding missing persons data, inclusivity of volunteer technology communities (including individuals who are not affiliated with any one particular group), refinement the PFIF community data standard, develop cross-walks with other emerging missing-person protocols like EDXL-TEP (now in the OASIS standardization process), create community governance of missing persons data by external actors such as volunteer technology communities, academia and the private sector, and encourage technical enhancements to the open source code.

Some Thoughts from a Software Development Perspective
By Glenn Pearson, Lost Person Finder Project, US National Library of Medicine

For system providers, working with evolving missing-person data-exchange standards is challenging, whether these are those that are de facto standards such as PFIF, or those undergoing formal consideration by a standards body, such as EDXL/TEP by OASIS. We are currently investigating the potential for cross-walks between these, and hope to report shortly to both communities. The trade-offs between timely but unfiltered public reporting, and reporting by trained responders, have been well-expressed by some of the other contributors to this statement.

Our system, "People Locator" (https://pl.nlm.nih.gov), derives from portions of the Sahana Disaster Management system, an open-source effort begun as a response to the 2006 Indonesian tsunami. We initially customized it towards the needs of a local Bethesda, Maryland, hospital consortium. In response to the Haiti earthquake the system was expanded in order to support international disasters. In particular, using PFIF, People Locator can readily and reliably import missing-person data from Google Person Finder repositories for subsequent searching. This capability was exercised most recently during the Tohoku disaster (shown), and further demonstrated at the ISCRAM 2011 InterOp Workshop in May.

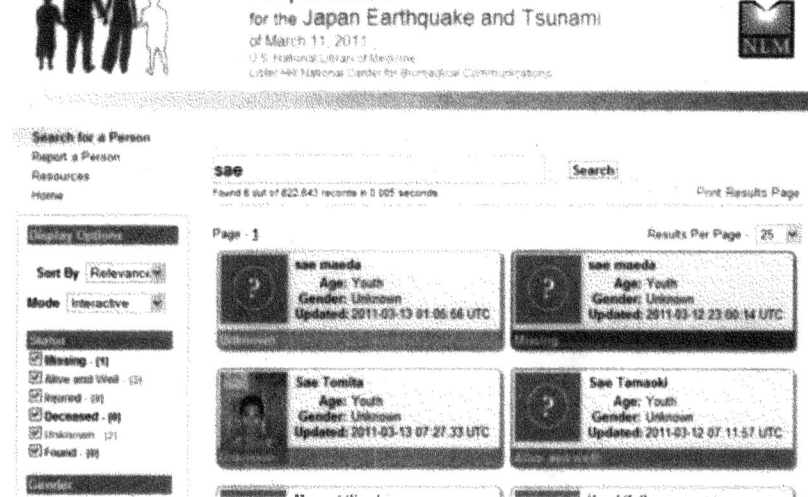

As an Institute within the National Institutes of Health, US National Library of Medicine (NLM) is very much aware of the concerns regarding individual privacy, patient confidentiality, and data lifetimes. For this project, while we work with Google, we do have differences of viewpoint in some of these matters and appreciate the role of CrisisCommons in providing an on-going venue for exploring these matters. In terms of shared goals, both Google, through their Google Summer of Code program and NLM through its internship programs, recognize the importance of engaging the next generation of computer-literate students in support of humanitarian response and emergency preparedness.

We have used social networking and volunteer response organizations like Sahana, Random Hacks of Kindness, and CrisisCommons, to help with web-site translations and new capabilities before and during disasters. We also foresee opportunities to make use of "crowd sourcing" to clarify and convert records. We continue our development of mobile apps such as our iPhone "ReUnite" to facilitate field reporting of those impacted by natural disasters.

Contributions to Attachment A provided from Glenn Pearson of the U.S. National Institute of Medicine, Heather Blanchard of CrisisCommons, Tim Schwartz, Google and Ka-Ping Yee.

Attachment B - Community Comment

In response to developing this Statement for Record, participants in the CrisisCommons community provided perspectives they wanted to share directly with the committee staff. These were collected through an open process where individuals and organizations choose whether to be cited or not.

Underscoring the Need for Training, Research and Resources
By Suzanne Frew, Pacific Disaster Resource Center

Pacific Disaster Center located in Kihei Hawaii works with decision makers, emergency managers, planners, and the public to develop solutions to some of the most challenging disaster management problems. The Pacific Disaster Center is working with Argonne National Lab and the University of Hawaii to research social media and disaster communications experiences between the 2010 and 2011 tsunami events. The Center has assisted United Nation agencies, national governments, relief organizations, and humanitarian assistance organizations in worldwide locations and works closely with Pacific Command to provide early warning and decision support tools, hazard modeling and visualization, risk and vulnerability assessment, training and exercise support. During the March 2011 Japan Earthquake/Tsunami the Pacific Disaster Center's website peaked to four times the traffic to 4.41 million hits with 77% of those visitors were looking for tsunami-specific content.

The Pacific Disaster Center believe that there are many opportunities where nongovernmental organizations use social media to fully utilize and distribute critical information such as preparedness campaigns that are resulting in excellent penetration of low-income areas and populations (minority, youth, etc.), gathering of rapid response intelligence from the population and rapid info distribution between networked preparedness and response organizations

In assessing the Federal government's role in the use of social media in emergency management, the Pacific Disaster Center recommends to Congress:
- Provide guidance to Federal government warning agencies to support and provide access to the related information, using a common protocol
- Provide grants and financing support to the existing networks to expand and promote use of social media through enhanced functionality and partnerships
- Facilitate and finance a social media strategy development and implementation process, inclusive of public, private and NGO, particularly emphasizing outreach to highly vulnerable populations.
- Integrate grant-based funding into current funding streams to Fed/S/L organizations to evolve partnership development targeting social media.
- Continue to expand National Science Foundation and National Institutes of Health funding for research (specifically, in information assurance for crowd-sourced data).
- Train emergency management staff and other key sectors in the proper utilization of social media for information sharing and data exchange, and promote social media use in the emergency management curriculum at universities and colleges.

The Pacific Disaster Center reflected on the potential for the maximization of resources recommends the following opportunities to better utilize public sector's tools:
- Utilize GIS and visualization techniques that can be pushed online for decision support,
- Provide grants and funding support for the integration of existing tools and technologies, including those for the mobile devices, that would facilitate information exchange, and

- Support the build of social media tools into the standard response go packages, preparedness guidance, and response annexes and protocols.

Social Media is helpful for Volunteers and Donation Management
By Jim Bass, Cecil County Emergency Management

Mr. Bass shared, "One of the greatest potential uses I see for social media in the wake of disasters is the advertisement of needs in regards to volunteers and donation. Platforms such as Facebook or Twitter are a fast and easy way to reach large groups and keep them informed of your needs, and such platforms also give a voice to the volunteer community in order to communicate what they plan to donate or how they plan to help."

Public/Private Partnerships
By Lloyd Colston, City of Altus (OK) Emergency Manager

Mr. Colston shared with CrisisCommons, "that public/private partnerships, as encouraged by Administrator Fugate, is in play in Oklahoma. The Oklahoma Crisis Mappers (http://www.oklahomacrisismappers.org/) has been involved in a number of winter weather events and, recently, fire weather events across the State. The citizen is able to get information, in a graphic form, mapped to their local area, with a link for additional text information that may be useful. The Oklahoma Crisis Mappers is an all-volunteer group with partnerships with local emergency managers and other government officials."

Social Media Fosters 2-Way Communication
By Alex Rose, CrisisCamp Southern California

Mr. Rose shared with CrisisCommons, "Social Media tools enable real-time 2-way communication channels that were not available to the disaster affected public or emergency managers just 2 years ago. And while Crisis Commons is an organization that is exploring how to more fully utilize these mediums, we recognize that agencies promoting use of social media must not make unsustainable commitments or establish inappropriate public expectations. While the public may turn to twitter to seek assistance during a disaster, if the local EMS, dispatch and 911 system is overwhelmed then those tweets will go unanswered. As the Federal Government joins forward-thinking groups like Crisis Commons we must all continue to promote the limits of our capabilities."

Social Media is Important for All Aspects of Emergency Management
By Pascal Schuback, CrisisCamp Seattle

Mr. Schuback shared with CrisisCommons, "These (social media) tools are important to the continued success of emergency management and its four phases, Planning, response, recovery and mitigation, that CrisisCommons continues to strive on a daily basis for the global communities. Just as we have accepted the use of email, 15+ years ago, social media tools and innovative projects will move us forward into building stronger resilient communities to future and unknown disasters."

Connecting Existing Resources at the Local Level
By Heather Blanchard, Co-Founder, CrisisCommons
From the August 12, 2010 presentation at the American Red Cross Crisis Data Summit
http://www.slideshare.net/poplifegirl/arc-08-12-10-final-short

Note: In Red are potential new functions, in black are existing roles

Potential Technology Cluster Model

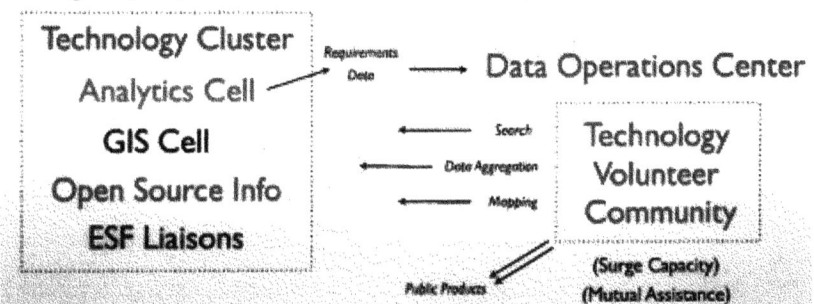

Opportunity for Mobile Disaster Assessments
By Willow Brugh, Geeks Without Bounds, Seattle, Washington

Ms. Brugh shared with CrisisCommons, "Creating a mobile assessment of damage for the public will make the process of assessing damage after catastrophe easier, quicker, and searchable. Will save hours for public employees, empower individuals, and speed recovery."

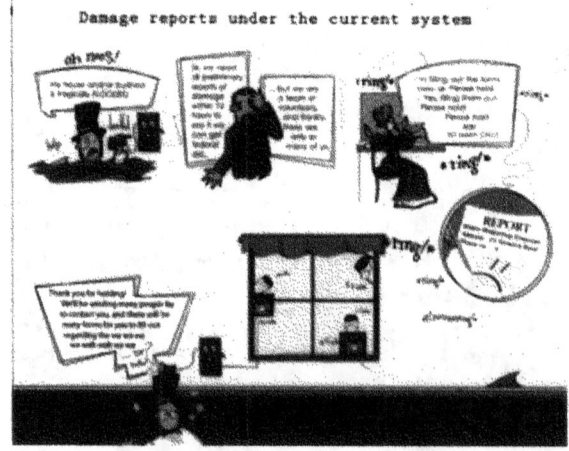

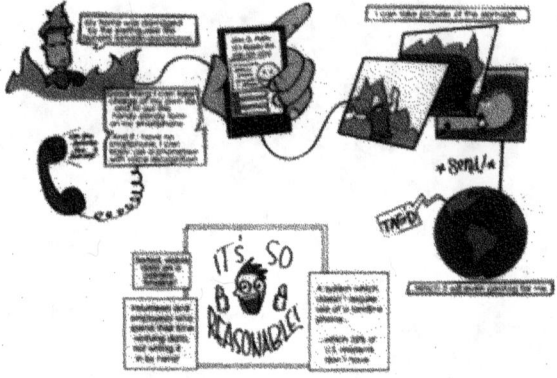

Opportunity in Location Based Check-In
By Teri Center, Silver Spring, Maryland

Ms. Center shared with CrisisCommons that the Department of State should figure out how to incorporate services like Life360 (http://www.life360.com/blog/over-1500-families-across-japan-use-life360s-safety-check-in-during-earthquake/) into their Smart Traveler Enrollment Program (https://travelregistration.state.gov/).

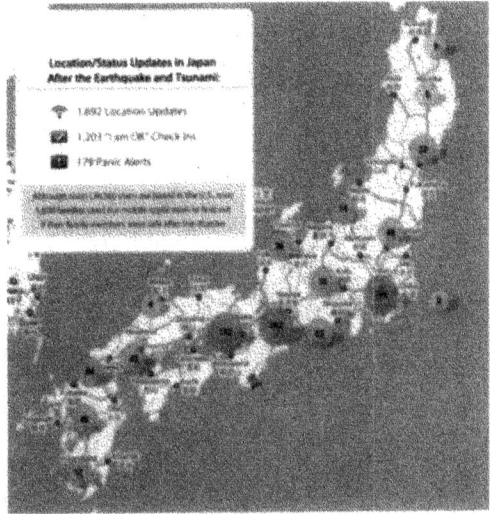

Could they also incorporate other location-based social media like FourSquare, GoWalla, and Facebook places? Could they allow people who plan to "check-in" anyway to "friend" STEP so that in case of a disaster in a certain location, they'd be able to quickly scan their list of registered users for recent check-ins at that location?

Role for Technology Volunteers
By Richard Barber, Morgan Hill, California

CrisisCommons has fostered the next generation of emergency management. It is an inclusive effort that can help bring together people during a crisis without regard to political division. Shortly after the massive flooding last year in Pakistan, I learned about a Crisis Camp occurring in my area. I was amazed to see and interact with the dozens of responders who gathered. Through online blogs, chats, and wikis, participants are linked across the globe, and efforts are very well organized.

One essential element of disaster management that I take very seriously is communications. As a fourth-generation amateur radio operator, I understand the need for rapid and accurate transmission of information. From the telegraph relay networks of our ancestors to today's satellite uplinks and downlinks, robust, reliable global communications systems will continue to play a vital role in emergency management. That's why I take special pride when a CrisisCommons supporter asks questions about Ham radio, and how radio communications works. Following the multiple disasters in Japan this March, I researched and reported on a CrisisCommons wiki page how Amateur Radio is being used, and could potentially be used in the crisis-stricken areas.

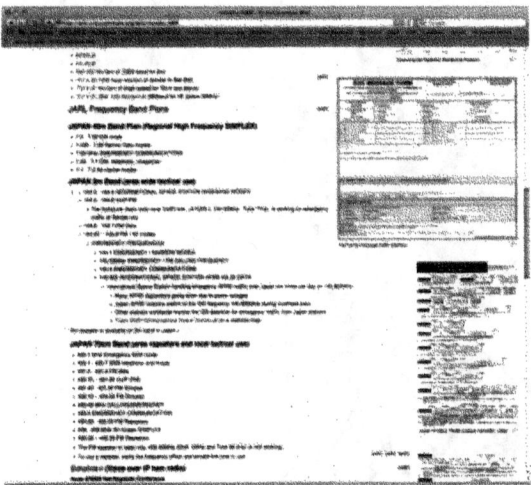

Other areas around the world have been suffering from ongoing humanitarian needs. Many people suffer as a result of perfect-storms of a combination of political mismanagement, agricultural ignorance, and long-standing civil strife. It is my own opinion that these people live in crisis also, and this opinion is represented by the requests of the United Nations Office of the Coordination of Humanitarian Affairs (UNOCHA) to CrisisCommons to provide support on behalf of the people affected by such perfect-storms. The prime example of such an area is Libya, but there are many others.

Often times we don't know if we can help, or if what we are capable of doing will help, but we always want to know that people are being helped, and we want to know that the people helping aren't missing anyone needing help. This need drives CrisisCommons participants to shift their attention from their daily routine to the plight of those suffering disaster, no matter where.

CrisisCommons is a serious and open effort. The people working on CrisisCommons projects do so because they care about the lives of those who suffer from disaster. I will continue to assist CrisisCommons in honor of those who have donated their valuable time and skills developing the technology and management practices that have become, in very short order, a model for existing and future communication organizations.

First Responder Communities of Practice
Anonymous Submission, Washington DC

The Department of Homeland Security Science and Technology Directorate First Responder Communities of Practice Website (www.communities.firstresponder.gov) is a vetted, professional networking, project collaboration, and resource-sharing platform for first responders and other personnel working in homeland security capacities. The site is focused on emergency response, preparedness, resiliency, planning, management, and homeland security-related matters. Site members can network with others in their fields and areas of interest; join or start new communities to collaborate "virtually" with others through wikis, blogs, discussion boards, real-time chat, and internal Website e-mail; find and share resources and contacts; store and access documents; and stay connected through e-mail notification of site activities. In addition to managing the site, the First Responder Communities of Practice Website also reports on the emergency response community's broader efforts to use social media to improve disaster preparedness and resilience.

DHS Working Group Recommends Social Media Best Practices

Anonymous Submission, Washington DC

DHS First Responder Communities of Practice recently launched the Virtual Social Media Working Group (VSMWG), which is comprised of first responders and homeland security professionals from various disciplines, localities, sectors, and government agencies across the country. The mission of the VSMWG is to provide recommendations to the emergency preparedness, response, and homeland security communities on the safe and sustainable use of social media technologies before, during, and after emergencies.

Members were selected by DHS First Responder Technologies (R-Tech) program based on their experience in leveraging social media technologies to pursue the missions of their agencies. Many VSMWG members have served as speakers, trainers, and subject matter experts at major homeland security-related workshops, roundtables, and conferences on the topic of social media. Representing the fields of emergency management, law enforcement, fire, emergency medical services, public health, public utilities, and local government, the VSMWG strives to be a dynamic voice in the social media and public safety arena, incorporating the perspectives of a wide range of stakeholders.

VSMWG members will collaborate via virtual meetings to identify and discuss responder issues and challenges with social media. They will look at myriad issues, such as standards and policies, and will provide recommended guidance on using social media in public safety. The working group may engage with subject matter experts from different sectors to work towards resolutions to these issues.

The First Responder Communities of Practice platform will serve as the primary location for the VSMWG to conduct activities, share developments, and connect with other homeland security professionals regarding the value of social media for emergency preparedness, response, and recovery. The group will play an active role in establishing the Make America Safer through Social Media Community on the First Responder Communities of Practice as a national resource for social media and public safety-related information and best practices.

"I don't trust FEMA, but I do trust Craig Fugate"
Marcus Deyerin, Bellingham, Washington

The value of social media for emergency management is in its dynamic nature, capacity for rapid adaptation, and general absence of critical nodes. These aren't things you can effectively "support" through legislation or regulation - but you sure can inhibit them (e.g. changes to net neutrality). Beware the hazard of unintended consequences [of ill-considered legislation].

Social media has changed the rules in regards to crisis communications. There's simply no such thing as "controlling" the message or information in general anymore. Just ask Hosni Mubarak. If government agencies (and individuals) want to be effective users of social media, they have to recognize they are an equal partner in the conversation, and the success or failure of any argument, direction, guidance, etc. will succeed or fail based not on being a "voice of authority" but rather the level of transparency and trust they have pre-established with their intended audience, which segues to...

Social media is about people - not faceless entities. Sure - you can have a "Department of X" Twitter account, but if it's written in government vanilla format - don't expect it to garner much attention. I don't "trust" FEMA - but I do trust Craig Fugate. Perhaps that isn't ideal - but it is what is.

Lastly, expect mistakes. Whether social media is evolutionary or revolutionary is debatable. What is less debatable is that our capacity to develop and adopt technology has far surpassed our cultural and sociological ability to comprehend the long-term ramifications of these technologies, for better and worse. The adoption of social media by government, corporations, and individuals has and will continue to provide ample opportunities to "cast the first stone." Therefore, social media missteps within the public sector should be evaluated with a certain degree of empathy, and judged along the full spectrum of maliciousness, stupidity, negligence, poor judgment, or simple ignorance, with responses appropriate to each.

Future Challenges and Opportunities
This anonymous submission was provided to CrisisCommons with citations from blog: http://headdowneyesopen.blogspot.com/2011/01/putting-power-into-hands-of-people-who.html

Here is a summarized version of what we can consider the main challenges/opportunities ahead if we are to truly be more effective at humanitarian aid by using available technologies to ensure people affected by disasters are more involved - that they become genuine partners in their own recovery. There are many more 'internal' institutional-type challenges which I won't go into here. If you feel some crucial points are omitted or contest those mentioned do join the discussion.

Some of these points are taken/inspired from a recent UN Dispatch blog post on a great new initiative that I'm sure will quickly become the basis for providing best practice, guidance and support for the aid community and communities affected by crises. Exciting times.

- Relevance: is information being received directly from people – including third party curators – relevant information that is actionable? Can we do something with the information or is it just wasting valuable time?

- Privacy: much of the personal information gathered by aid workers in the course of their duties is personal and confidential information. In some contexts, more than we might imagine, such information needs to be treated with utmost sensitivity and confidentiality. Protocols on the handling of personal data gathered and disseminated by SMS technologies (for instance but others too) should be developed much in the way confidentiality is practiced by the time-tested protocols of the ICRC's Tracing Agency.

- Verification: is the information accurate? Is it true? Is it a ruse? Could it create a security problem?

- Duplication: are we the only ones who received the info? Is someone else dealing with it? Do we need (yet again) new coordination mechanisms?

- Access: do the people who own the aid outcomes i.e. the most vulnerable people, do they have access to the information channels created by new technologies, better use of SMS portals etc?

- Expectations: Are we creating excessively high expectations which we will not be able to manage? That is, by gathering so much date and info from people are we contributing to a misperception that all these needs will be addressed?

- Proximity: Mobile technologies and satellite communications are bringing everyone—humanitarian organizations, international institutions, volunteer technical communities, and the affected populations —ever closer together. More often than not, victims of disasters and conflicts have cell phones and can communicate via SMS in real time.

- Speed: As a result, information flows are accelerating, raising expectations around increasing the tempo of information management and coordination in emergency operations.

- Duality: At the same time, the methods for data and information exchange are moving from document-based systems to flows of structured data via web services. This movement from the narration of ongoing events in long stretches of unstructured prose to streams of data in short semi-structured formats require humanitarian staff to perform double duty. They are simultaneously working within an existing system based on the exchange of situation reports while filtering and analyzing high volumes of short reports arriving via SMS and web services.

Conflict and disaster management in a hyperconnected world - cooperative, collaborative, real-time
By Stephen Collins, Australia
Source: http://acidlabs-cdn.s3.amazonaws.com/Conflict%20and%20disaster%20management%20in%20a%20hyperconnected%20world.pdf

In Australia, the US, the UK and elsewhere, including on a multinational/UN basis, there are painfully few examples of truly skilled individuals and agencies with an official civil-military remit using social and collaborative technologies in either disaster or conflict management. Nor are they actively participating in networks of expertise and collaborating with them in order to improve their capacity to act.

A number of events are already taking place around the region; events the civil-military community are not engaging with. These include Bridging the Gap Think Tank, in Sydney on 21 May and the global Random Hacks of Kindness (RHoK) in 16 locations around the world in early June.29 Not actively participating in these events represents a singular missed opportunity for the civil-military sector. Many Australian organisations across the conflict and disaster management community are now increasingly aware of the value of the use of social technologies and hyperconnectivity to improve the way they work, including during times of crisis. Several agencies, including the Attorney-General's Department have signalled they intend to investigate these approaches and a number of events to discuss experiences, research and views have been held.30 Investigation, however, is not enough.

There is more than adequate academic and organisational research and use-in-practice evidence to show that organisations involved in official civil-military response gain measurable insight and response capability, even in the face of emergent, rapidly changing and significantly complex events when they engaged and working with technologically adept networked communities such as CrisisMappers and SBTF. In the words of GFDRR manager, Saroj Kumar Jha:

> "The use of Volunteer Technology Communities (VTCs) made possible by new Web 2.0 technologies present a fundamental shift in how we can support Disaster Risk Management programs and intervene in disaster situations. We are only at the beginning of this story. The seeds planted through initiatives like the Crisis Commons and Random Hacks of Kindness hold great promise for the future."

Australian civil-military agencies, and in all likelihood their equivalents elsewhere need to act to improve their capacity to engage with networked communities around crisis and disaster management.
To build skills and knowledge, as the US State Department is doing in at home and globally, so too DFAT, the Department of Defence and AusAID could actively engage with the volunteer technical communities, building relationships and expertise on both sides.

H605-41331-79W7 with DISTILLER

An international research effort as well as events akin to RHoK and CrisisCamp, should be sponsored by civil-military organisations such as the Asia-Pacific Civil-Military Centre of Excellence and their international peers. This activity would explicitly seek to involve the various communities - VTCs, academia, the innovation sector, CrisisCommons, The Standby Task Force and others - with an aim of fostering good working relationships and incorporating culture change, tools and practices and lessons learned with respect to the inclusion of networked communities in disaster and conflict response into civil-military doctrine by July 2012.

Building trust and strong relationships is an important first step. These actions could facilitate collaboration between the official and volunteer actors in the civil-military, disaster management and crisis response sectors, would improve knowledge amongst all involved and would certainly improve the capacity to respond effectively and efficiently to events in the future.

More than two-thirds agree that response agencies should regularly monitor and respond to postings on their websites.

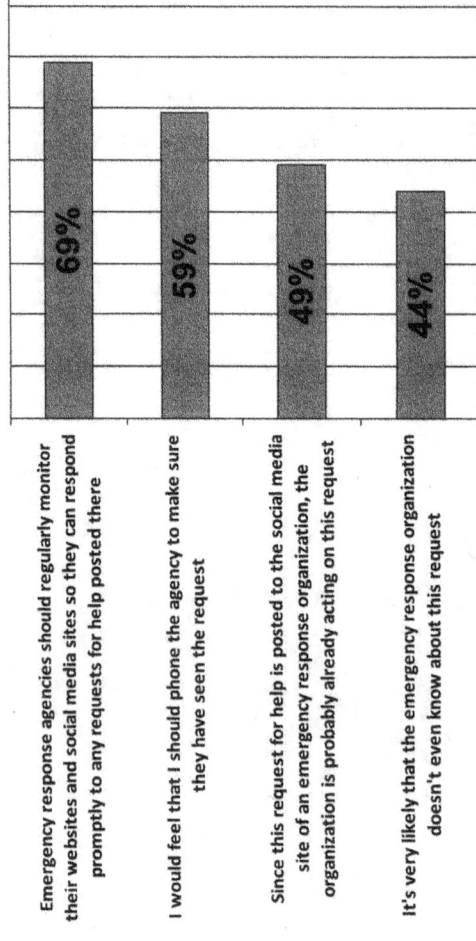

- Emergency response agencies should regularly monitor their websites and social media sites so they can respond promptly to any requests for help posted there — **69%**

- I would feel that I should phone the agency to make sure they have seen the request — **59%**

- Since this request for help is posted to the social media site of an emergency response organization, the organization is probably already acting on this request — **49%**

- It's very likely that the emergency response organization doesn't even know about this request — **44%**

13 Imagine that you are on a social media site for an emergency response organization such as FEMA or the American Red Cross and you see a recent post that includes an urgent request for help. To what extent do you agree or disagree with the following statements? (Percentages indicate Strongly Agree and Agree)

American Red Cross

Google Search Query Volume Post-Disaster
The Internet still works after most disasters – and victims use it to search for information.

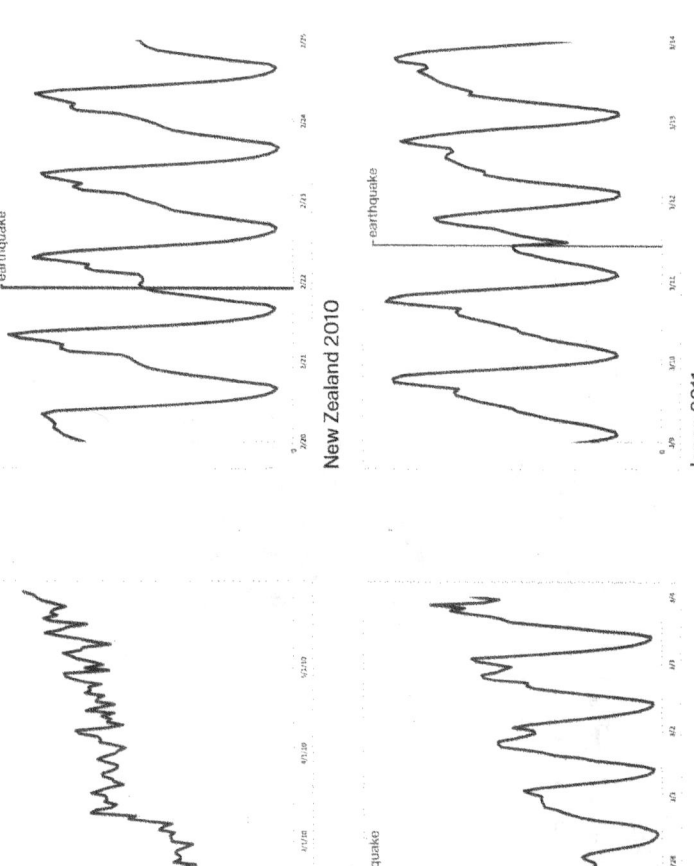

Haiti 2010

Chile 2010

New Zealand 2010

Japan 2011

☐3

During an emergency, nearly half would use social media to let loved ones know they are safe.

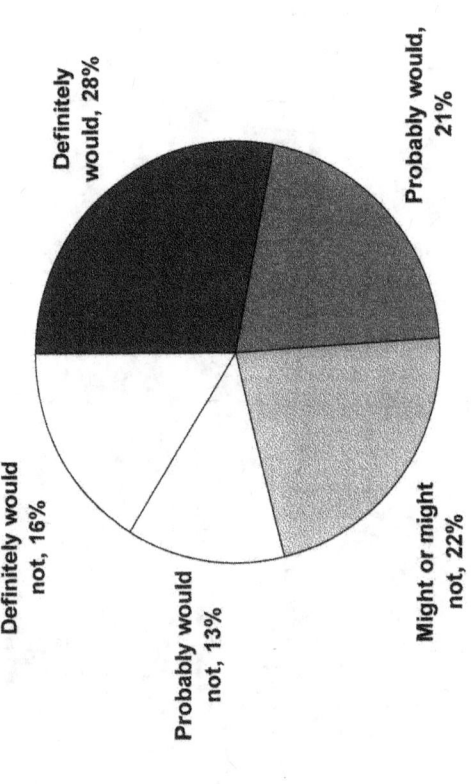

Definitely would, 28%

Probably would, 21%

Might or might not, 22%

Probably would not, 13%

Definitely would not, 16%

In an area-wide emergency, how likely would you be to use social media channels to let your friends and family know you are safe?

American Red Cross

11

Post-Hearing Questions for the Record
Submitted to Craig W. Fugate, Administrator, FEMA
From Senator Mark L. Pryor

"Understanding the Power of Social Media as a Communications Tool in the Aftermath of Disasters"
May 5, 2011

1. What are FEMA's goals for its use of social media tools? Are there any agency performance metrics associated with FEMA's goals for the use of social media tools?

   Response: FEMA uses social media as a way to engage the public as an emergency management resource. To that end, our ultimate goal is to maximize two-way communication, sharing information with state and local government as well as the public, but also enabling these parties to share information with us.

   FEMA has established performance metrics for social media. On a quarterly basis, we measure the number of people we are reaching through digital engagement by tracking the number of visitors to our website and mobile site, the number of fans and followers we have on Facebook and Twitter, and the number of individuals who subscribe to our emails. However, while these performance metrics can be useful in certain circumstances, they are subjective measures and do not account for the level of active engagement of individuals. We will continue working to ensure that not only are we reaching as many individuals as possible through social media and digital channels, but that we are maximizing the engagement of those individuals.

2. We know that social media networks often reach out to FEMA and other disaster agencies during times of crisis. However, they are often frustrated to find that there is no single point of contact they can communicate with disaster after disaster. What steps need to be taken to make social media outreach a standardized process?

   Response: FEMA has clear points of contact for social media networks in both FEMA's Private Sector Division as well as FEMA's Public Affairs Division. We communicate closely as needed before, during, and after a disaster. No social media network has raised this frustration with FEMA.

3. As we discussed at the hearing, the use of the internet as a tool of choice during disasters is likely to continue to grow. What is the government's role in fostering greater collaboration to ensure that social media is truly the two-way communication tool we hope it can be?

   Response: The Federal Emergency Management Administration's (FEMA) primary mission is to *support* our citizens and first responders to ensure that as a nation we work together to build, sustain, and improve our capability to prepare for, protect against, respond to, recover from, and mitigate all hazards. That support mission applies in the social media context as well.

H605-41331-79W7 with DISTILLER

In the aftermath of the 2009 flooding in Tennessee, we worked with the Tennessee Emergency Management Agency (TEMA) and set up a joint Facebook page that we used as a resource to provide the public with the latest information about ongoing disaster response and recovery efforts in Tennessee. Now that the main recovery phase has concluded, TEMA uses the Facebook page as its own means to share preparedness and disaster-related information.

FEMA also partnered with the Alabama Emergency Management Agency to create a joint Facebook page as an additional way to reach Alabama residents during the response and recovery efforts after the recent severe storms and tornadoes. We will continue to use our social media resources as a way to further that support.

4. Are there barriers to greater and more effective use of these tools that currently exist in the Federal government? Can you provide specific examples, such as barriers or gaps that exist because of existing Federal laws, regulations, or bureaucratic silos across Federal agencies?

Response: As is the case with any new and emerging technology, we will continue to learn how to use social media tools more effectively. Social media in the emergency management context is a shared effort among government, private sector, and the individuals who use these tools in order to define how we communicate with one another before, during, and after a disaster occurs. We continue to grow our understanding of how to use social media to its greatest potential.

5. At the hearing we heard about the challenge we face in enhancing digital literacy and placing vital information in a universal open forum. Where do FEMA and DHS stand on making progress in meeting those goals? What resources does FEMA need to help coordinate and aggregate this information in a way that will make it accessible to everyone?

a. Your testimony mentioned that you have encouraged your governmental and private sector collaborators to "free the data" and make information like evacuation routes and shelter locations more easily accessible. Are there staff engaged in oversight of that process? Do you have a sense of what resources might help this goal along?

Response: Our challenge lies not in enhancing digital literacy among the communities we serve, but rather, adapting to the way the public communicates. To that end, we use social media outlets like Facebook and Twitter, and other digital channels, like the FEMA blog and FEMA's mobile website, as tools in our toolkit. Of course, in order to ensure that we are able to communicate information in a way that is accessible to everyone, we utilize both newer technologies like social media as well as more traditional mechanisms for conveying information, like press releases, print media, town halls and through our community relations teams in a disaster environment.

FEMA has a small, dedicated digital engagement staff working to ensure that we are able to share relevant disaster information with the individuals who use social media and other digital tools. In 2007, FEMA established a Private Sector Division of External Affairs. Our Private Sector Division facilitates full engagement with business and industry, academia, non-profit and other non-governmental organizations as key players in disaster preparedness, response, and recovery. Our increased communication and coordination with the private sector has helped and will continue to help us share relevant information with the individuals and communities we serve.

□□

Post-Hearing Questions for the Record
Submitted to Renee Preslar, Public Information Officer, ADEM
From Senator Mark L. Pryor

"Understanding the Power of Social Media as a Communications Tool in the Aftermath of Disasters"
May 5, 2011

1. You testified as to the presence of local Offices of Emergency Management (OEMs) on Facebook as a way to work around the limited resources available for establishing a website. Is there oversight in place to make sure that the gaps in this presence are closing?

   I am not aware of any oversight in place to make sure the gaps in this presence are closing.

a. What feedback have you received from local OEMs on this shift? Are there consistent requests they have made or concerns they have expressed?

   Of the OEMs that participate in social sites, they are pleased with the opportunity and platform it gives them to have conversations with those in their community; even with some that do have websites because the websites are static and not very easy to change, whereas they can update the social sites as often as they choose.

   They have expressed a few concerns. One of which is personnel. They have found that there is not a lot of ability to converse with citizens when they are in the field working. Another concern is how to that at this time the channels are not for emergency notification. They use them as preparedness outreach and if time is available they post weather warnings and some recovery. Because job responsibilities take them into the field during response and often recovery of disasters, there is no one present to monitor feed that may come in at that time. So currently there is no way to monitor feeds that may come in during the response phase from citizens that need help. Because of this they make sure they express that they will not always be available to monitor the feed and comment.

2. The response process you discuss in terms of creating an update within 15 minutes of learning of a situation is an interesting adaptation to our changing technology. Is there a procedure allowing you to filter these down through the relevant local OEM?

   The update that is created within 15 minutes is simply a way of adapting to the changing technology. It does not go into detail about specifics because within that short time frame it is often difficult to fully understand the specifics of a situation. What it does is let citizens know you are aware of the event and responding as needed, even if you do not give details about the response at that time. Waiting a few hours before issuing the first comments about a situation gives the impression that nothing was being done until then, even though that is the exact opposite of what was happening. This way, when you do have specifics an hour or two in to an event, this is not the first time the public has heard from you.

   Local OEMs have the ability to do this as well; however as was previously mentioned concerns, it is not always possible.

Post-Hearing Questions for the Record
Submitted to Suzy DeFrancis, Chief Public Affairs Officer, American Red Cross
From Senator Mark L. Pryor

"Understanding the Power of Social Media as a Communications Tool in the Aftermath of Disasters"
May 5, 2011

1. Is there a need for a separate, common database of disaster related information that can be utilized by the different social media outlets and the Federal Government alike to access and share certain types of disaster specific data?
   a. What privacy concerns exist over the sharing of disaster-related data?
   b. How can we avoid privacy violations as we seek to foster greater access to this information?

   Answer:
   Yes. A single aggregator for disaster related information, would be instrumental in disaster response efforts. However, creating and executing such a database may be difficult to achieve if we first don't quickly and successfully connect social media to disaster response and relief agencies. As I mentioned during the hearing, people who are in a crisis will turn to the most comfortable communication tools, including social media. Unfortunately, there is a gap between the number of individuals depending on social media and the amount of staff at disaster response and relief agencies ready to act on these messages.

   The American Red Cross fully understands the importance of protecting private information shared by individuals during times of disaster. And, I appreciate the Senator recognizing the importance of protecting privacy when sharing disaster-related data. If the database transmits publicly posted emergency social data the concern for privacy is minimal. Nevertheless, as social media becomes more integrated into our disaster response efforts, the need for ensuring privacy must continue to be part of the conversations.

2. Your NSS application utilizes Google Maps to aggregate shelter data. There seems to be significant overlap of purpose and format of your Safe and Well website and Google's Person Finder. Has there been information sharing or collaboration between your organizations to pool these resources?

   Answer:
   Yes. The American Red Cross Safe & Well team and Google have been talking about the interoperability of data. Our challenge is identifying a third party to help develop an interoperability standard. As these conversations continue, the American Red Cross is ever mindful of protecting data and information provided by those who access the Safe & Well website during times of disaster. We strive to achieve that balance between protecting the privacy of users and sharing data.

There is a third party volunteer technology group, currently called "Missing Persons Group" who developed a data standard called PFIF. We are now exploring how Safe & Well can collaborate with this data standard and Google Person Finder to share missing persons information more efficiently.

3. Your white papers on the uses of social media describes many ways that information is a) pushed out to the public, but also b) ways that all the information coursing through these information networks can be collected and analyzed to improve situational assessment and awareness. Can you provide more information on which tools your agency uses to enhance your response and recovery efforts?

Answer:
The most important tools we use are the ears and eyes of our staff and volunteers to listen to incoming information as soon as disasters happen.

We frequently use tools such as Facebook, Twitter, and Google both to message important information and to filter and collect social data pertaining to disasters. Many of us also use third party applications to help filter the vast amount of information: Tweetdeck, Hootsuite, Swift River, and Thrive are several examples.

Additionally, we use paid social monitoring software platform Radian6 to filter, aggregate, engage, and respond to incoming data from all social tools. We've recently begun using the Radian6 engagement console and we hope to share information with specially identified digital volunteers to help us filter and present this vast data to our shared operations.

We are also beginning to utilize a new tool developed by one of our vendors, VisionLink. This tool allows us to pull in various data resources, to include social media and photos, on to a shared mapping platform. This tool is designed to be access by relief workers to integrate and filter social media input (as well as other factors such as shelters and damage boundaries) into service delivery planning.

2

Questions for the Record
Submitted to Shona Brown, Senior Vice President, Google.org
From Senator Mark L. Pryor
Homeland Security Ad Hoc Subcommittee on Disaster Recovery and
Intergovernmental Affairs

"Understanding the Power of Social Media as a Communications Tool in the
Aftermath of Disasters"
May 5, 2011

1. Both your testimony and the briefing that Google's Crisis Response Team
put together were extremely insightful. Google explained very thoroughly that
it hopes to be an open resource and to become a one-stop shop bringing
together resources from different sites so that when disaster survivors search
for information, they get the consistent information no matter where they go.

a. How does Google verify the information it compiles?

We are unable to validate the accuracy of the information on crowdsourced tools at the time
it's posted in an automated way, and our tools would be less useful if we delayed information
from being surfaced to review it manually. For example, Person Finder is largely valuable for
the immediacy by which people can find and post information about their loved ones. That
does mean that people will sometimes post incorrect information. We continue to do our
best to remove such posts when flagged, and largely rely on users input.

We're at an early stage of understanding how best to utilize crowd sourced information, but
it is a powerful source in times of crisis. With Person Finder we have numerous anecdotes
and data on usage to show this has been helpful.

Other sources, such as government and relief agencies, are considered authoritative sources,
and we will direct users to those sources or incorporate their data into our alerts.

b. How does the company source information, especially information that directs disaster survivors to resources and locations?

Google's crisis response tools use information from a number of sources, some of which
are considered authoritative and others that rely on first responders and those experiencing

the crisis first-hand. We believe both these sources to be important for crisis response tools and our goal to make tools, and information, available quickly.

One example of how we go about finding information and using it in our crisis response tools is Resource Finder, a web application used to disseminate information about health facilities and the services they offer, which may change rapidly during a disaster. The application is designed to work for a variety of types of resources, and our first use case is for health facility resources. Resource Finder can help relief workers find up-to-date information on services, equipment, and beds available at neighboring health facilities so that they can efficiently arrange patient transfers.

Several organizations have been using Resource Finder as trusted testers in Haiti and now in Pakistan, both sharing information with us and pointing us towards information that we should incorporate in order to make Resource Finder more effective. Currently, Resource Finder has data imported from Google Map Maker and provided by Naya Jeevan, a non-profit organization working to provide access to affordable healthcare in Pakistan. Additionally, anyone working at a medical facility in the impact area can go to Resource Finder and add/update information about their health facility.

In the emergency context, Google Earth, Google Maps, and Google MapMaker help organizations visualize assets geographically and make it easier for the affected population to find nearby emergency resources. We work with governments, NGOs, intergovernmental organizations, and relief organizations in order to update these images.

This allows for quick damage assessments from thousands of miles away and can help relief organizations navigate disaster zones with, for example, crowdsourced information on available roads. Other tools like People Finder also rely on users to share information with each other.

c. How can Google work with government agencies and other social media outlets to ensure that it is always pushing accurate information?

In order to make the Internet more useful for those impacted by crises, companies and governments can both improve how they share information during crisis response situations. One way to make information sharing much easier is to use standard data formats, thus enabling all responders - whether no matter their organization - to easily and quickly find and use the information they need. Currently, companies and governments often use divergent data standards, slowing collaboration and response time because information cannot be shared. Ensuring that compatible, open standards are used across the board will enable users, government, and companies to share and communicate information.

As we mentioned in our testimony, to pursue some of the projects we undertake, Google had to gather emergency information from government websites in arcane formats and then translate them into open standards. Sometimes the information was spread across numerous websites. Other times, the licensing status of the data was not readily apparent. And even today, some important data is not even online at all, but rather is kept in a spreadsheet on a personal computer.

We recommend adoption of better alerting systems that leverage the Common Alerting Protocol (CAP) standard to quickly inform users of impending crises such as tsunamis and everyday alerts including transit delays.

> **2. Is there a need for a separate, common database of disaster related information that can be utilized by the different social media outlets and the Federal government alike to access and share certain types of disaster specific data?**

>> **a. What privacy concerns exist over the sharing of disaster-related data?**

Some information that is shared in the event of a crisis is necessarily about people. However, we take a great deal of care to make it clear to users that information they share will be made public.

>> **b. How can we avoid privacy violations as we seek to foster greater access to this information?**

A database of disaster related information for use by social media outlets could be very useful for disaster response efforts. At Google, we already try to bring together a number of publicly available information sources.

Tools like People Finder rely on users entering information about the people that they may be concerned about, or that they have information to share about that person. All records in Person Finder are available to the public. Users are not required to submit age information about individuals they are searching for, and Google does not verify the accuracy of the information submitted. The records have always been publicly available to make it easier to find people you care about. We've found, however, that this kind of data is most useful immediately after a crisis and becomes less useful as time passes. Out of respect for our users, we don't want to publish or keep this information longer than is necessary. Users can specify when they want a record to expire: it will automatically disappear from Google Person Finder at that time, and it will be gone from our backups within 60 days thereafter. Users can also delete a record at any time.

Our goal is to provide a tool with basic search functionality to allow people to locate their loved ones. We make it clear that any information shared using this tool is publicly available, and we consider these to be best practices for this kind of crisis response tool.

3. The social media tools we discussed at the hearing have been also referred to as "Web 2.0." What are some of the new applications that will further assist in emergency management and response?

> **a. What does the future entail? Is there a "Web 3.0" and what will it bring to assist in disaster preparedness, response and recovery?**

While we cannot predict the future of the Internet and tools for crisis response, we believe that location-based services and mobile services are promising technologies. These services allow responders to tailor their alerts and services to those directly affected by an event. Mobile devices also allow very specific information for first responders, and tools are being developed by government and third parties to more effectively allow responders to find relevant information.

> **4. You discussed the opportunity presented by the development of IPAWS as a source point to pull together critical information during disasters. Can you provide more information about what Google would like to see from IPAWS as it is developed?**

The Integrated Public Alert and Warning System, or IPAWS, is a plan to expand the traditional Emergency Alert System to include more modern technologies (including sending messages to cell phones with the Commercial Mobile Alert System). This program is a great first step in ensuring that information is shared in the event of a crisis, integrating data government agencies and others to allow for a robust Internet-based warning system. Notably, IPAWS is one of the early adopters of the CAP protocol for alerting.

With this kind of interoperable and open alerting systems and protocols, private actors such as Google will be able to interact with government systems to display alerts tailored to the geography, vulnerability, and situation around a crisis. Because this is open, any other Internet company or emergency organization can use or build on it quickly, when needed. These collaborative relationships will be able to provide emergency evacuation routes based on location, or other alerts as necessary during a crisis. Ensuring that these alerting agencies have the resources to move to simple, standard and open reporting formats will improve and speed disaster recovery and relief in the future.

Questions for the Record
Submitted to Shona Brown, Senior Vice President, Google.org
From Senator Joseph I. Lieberman
Homeland Security Ad Hoc Subcommittee on Disaster Recovery
and Intergovernmental Affairs

"Understanding the Power of Social Media as a Communications Tool in the
Aftermath of Disasters"
May 5, 2011

1. The Committee recently released an investigative report entitled A Ticking Time
Bomb: Counterterrorism Lessons from the U.S. Government's Failure to Prevent the
Fort Hood Attack. The report stated, "In the past, face-to-face interactions were
essential for violent Islamist extremist groups to identify followers and to facilitate
the radicalization process. However, face-to-face interactions have begun to be
replaced by the internet as the primary means by which violent Islamist extremism
has spread globally. Al Qaeda and other violent Islamist extremists recognized the
potency of the internet after 9/11 when they created a relatively structured, online
media campaign that targeted western audiences. Over time, violent Islamist
extremists have continued to evolve and improve their ability to use the Web to
broadcast the ideology. Their violent propaganda has spread from password
protected forums to include "mainstream" sites."

These mainstream sites include YouTube, which in recent years, has become a
primary communication tool for al Qaeda and its ideological allies to spread their
message. In November 2010, YouTube instituted a "flag" for videos which "promote
terrorism."

    a. How is YouTube promoting this new terrorism flag to its users? Please
    give specific examples.

YouTube's flagging menu contains a number of labels to help users identify and flag material that
violates our Guidelines. Our users choose flagging categories like "violent or repulsive content" and
"hateful or abusive content" to identify this type of content and bring it to our attention. To make it
even easier for our users to identify material that incites violence, in November 2010 we added a flag
labeled "promoting terrorism" to the menu, which appears directly below every one of the hundreds
of millions of videos on YouTube. At the time of the addition we briefed numerous reporters about
the new flagging option. To help our users understand how the flag should be used, we added further
details about the new flag to the YouTube Help Center.

b. YouTube's Terms of Service (ToS) were updated to expressly prohibit terrorist content. Will Google update its overarching ToS and other specific ToS, such as that for Blogspot, to accord with YouTube's ToS?

Blogger's policies prohibit threatening content, content that promotes "dangerous and illegal activities," contains hate speech, or inciteful material that encourages "violent action against another person or group of people." Similar to YouTube, when material of this nature is reported to Blogger, review teams take action to remove the content quickly.

c. How many videos have been flagged for promoting terrorism since YouTube instituted this flag on a monthly basis? How many videos have been removed as a result of this flag on a monthly basis?

YouTube users flag thousands of videos every day, and our global policy enforcement team reviews content around the clock, routinely removing material that violates our policies. While we don't comment publicly on flagging volumes, we can confirm that the promotes terrorism flag, as well as other flags for violence and hateful content, are being actively used by our community to bring potentially inciteful content to our enforcement team's attention.

d. Does YouTube proactively scan its site for terrorist content? If so, how many videos are taken down on a monthly basis (on average over the last twelve months) as a result?

Video is uploaded you YouTube at the rate of 35 hours per minute. Because of the massive scale of the platform, it is not possible to pre-screen content. To ensure that our policies are followed, we have a community policing system in place whereby users report prohibited material by selecting the "Flag" link under every video. Our policy review team reviews flagged videos 24 hours a day, seven days a week, removing material that violates our Guidelines. In addition, we have a Help & Safety Tool that lets users contact us about threatening comments. A staff of specialists is on hand around the clock taking action to remove and, when appropriate, report such comments.

e. Once the videos are flagged, a YouTube employee reviews the content to make a final decision on removal.

i. Are there specific guidelines for removal of content that promotes terrorism? If so, please provide them.

Every video flagged for our attention is reviewed for violations of our Community Guidelines, and material found to be in violation is promptly removed. YouTube's Guidelines prohibit users from uploading videos or posting comments that contain hate speech and threats of violence against specific individuals or groups. We also prohibit videos that promote dangerous or illegal activities (including bomb-making, sniper attacks, or other terrorist acts), and videos that are posted with the purpose of inciting others to commit specific, serious acts of violence. In addition, we remove all videos and terminate any account registered by a member of a designated Foreign Terrorist Organization (FTO) and used in an official capacity to further the interests of the FTO.

Material is reviewed carefully, and videos that do not violate those policies will remain on the site. In addition, we necessarily carve out exceptions for educational and documentary content, for example the thousands of videos posted by our partners in the news media.

2

ii. What type of training on terrorist ideology and propaganda do YouTube reviewers receive?

Keeping YouTube safe for our users is extremely important to us. Our policy enforcement team undergoes regular training, and we are in regular communication with third-party experts and organizations on a broad range of policy issues.

f. Do you believe that other leading companies with social media platforms, such as Facebook and Twitter, should institute such self-flagging specifically for terrorism- related content?

We don't comment on the policies or enforcement practices of other companies.

2. Industry plays a vital role in preventing violent radicalization. We have seen in the youth-driven uprisings in the Arab world that social media can be a catalyst for positive change. In many ways, Google is on the forefront of the war of ideas against violent Islamist extremism. Many Muslim Americans are fighting the ideological message of al Qaeda online but lack the technical know-how to compete on the same level of sophistication of the well-tuned al Qaeda messaging apparatus.

a. How is Google empowering those positive voices within Muslim American communities to counter messages against violent Islamist extremism?

Google has sought out and worked with groups and individuals who lead Muslim American communities in order to better educate them about using technology to project their messages. Working with personnel from key government agencies and the New America Foundation, we have provided training on Google tools and services, as well as those of other companies. We demonstrate this by showing examples of non-profit groups from many areas that have successfully taken advantage of Google tools and services. We have not worked directly on the content of the message but focused rather on increasing the groups' audience and the range of the tools they can use.

b. Does Google provide technical assistance on a *regular* basis to groups fighting this ideology?

In February, 2011, Google and Facebook co-sponsored at Google's office the first technical assistance session for these groups. Google, YouTube and Facebook personnel provided in-depth instruction in the use of tools ranging from our non-profit services to mapping technology to video to analytics (which allows a group to see who is visiting their site). In concert with other companies, Google is working on a plan that would provide more regular technical assistance to these groups and individuals.

c. Does Google provide "best practices" to such Muslim American groups for effectively promoting their messages online?

See above.

d. Is Google planning to provide and additional assistance to such Muslim American groups?

3

H605-4133I-79W7 with DISTILLER

See above. Note that Google is one of a handful of companies that, under the auspices of the New America Foundation, has pledged to play a technical and financial role in the development of a campaign against violent extremism that includes Muslim American groups and others.

3. Google's think tank, Google Ideas, and the Council on Foreign Relations will host a conference soon which brings together academics, policy makers, and former radicals to discuss how to prevent violent extremism. I commend Google Ideas for being proactive in this manner.

a. News reports state this conference will be the first step in a continued process by Google Ideas to counter violent extremism. How will Google Ideas engage with Americans, specifically Muslim Americans, who are actively trying to counter radicalization within their communities?

Google Ideas is organized by focus area and one of its four priorities for 2011 is countering violent extremism. June 26-28, Google Ideas will partner with CFR to convene 80 former gang members, former religious extremists, former nationalist extremists, and former right-wing extremists. For the purposes of the conference, "former" is defined by those who left the group, renounced violence, and are now actively and publicly working against the groups they used to be part of. In addition to the formers, Google Ideas and CFR are also inviting 15 survivors of terrorism and violence as well as roughly 110 NG Os, academics, public sector officials (including from House and Senate Homeland Security Committees), and private sector representatives, who are working on countering violent extremism issues. Some of these organizations already work closely with the Muslim American community, but our goal is to connect the credible voices -- formers and survivors -- with those in the American and international Muslim communities so they can forge partnerships in an effort to counter violent extremism together.

b. Has Google or Google Ideas considered providing private funding to groups countering the message of violent Islamist extremism?

At present, Google Ideas is not a grant giving organization. However, we do believe that Google Ideas is making a valuable contribution by investing in the convening of this network. Google Ideas is also working to build a web platform, anti-extremism campaign, and several products to support the efforts of those credible voices working against violent extremism. We are also building a Formers YouTube channel, which will allow credible voices like ex-extremists and survivors of terrorism to upload videos condemning violence and speaking out against terrorism.

Responses to Questions for the Record
Heather Blanchard, Co Founder, CrisisCommons
July 7, 2011

Responses to "Questions for the Record Submitted by Senator Mark L. Pryor to Heather
Blanchard, Co Founder of CrisisCommons from the May 5, 2011 hearing, "Understanding the
Power of Social Media as a Communications Tool in the Aftermath of Disasters"

1. You mentioned in your testimony that it is important to move toward more participatory
crisis management. Can you elaborate on what that means and why it is so important?

Response: Henry Jenkins, USC Annenberg School, provides potentially the best definition of
participatory culture in the MacArthur Foundation Report entitled Confronting the Challenges of
Participatory Culture:[1]

> *"A culture with relatively low barriers to artistic expression and civic engagement,*
> *strong support for creating and sharing one's creations and some type of informal mentorship*
> *whereby what is known by the most experienced is passed along to novices." He goes on*
> *to share, "Within participatory culture members believe their contributions matter and*
> *feel some degree of social connection with one another (at the least they care what other*
> *people think about what they have created)."*

Within the context of participatory culture sense, we term the growing interest and willingness of
citizens to support response efforts as the rise of a "Crisis Crowd" which, from our experience,
appears when there is interest and ability to self-organize (usually via the Internet). These are
everyday people, who know no geographic limitation, who step forward and want to help support
communities in crisis. These individuals often have valuable in-kind expertise and resources with
the emergency response community, sharing access to such resources as Web servers or
language translation, which they are willing to contribute as in-kind resource. People are
offering their time, which has a monetary value. However, the many of these skills and assets
remain used or "left on the table" because these individuals and ad hoc volunteer networks are
uncertain where they can effectively donate their skills and resources in an effective and
meaningful way. The emergency management community, in turn, is unsure of how to integrate
these volunteer efforts into traditional response procedures.

To effectively harness the considerable skills and resources these volunteer communities offer,
emergency management need have developed a plan for coordinating with these skills and
resources. During a crisis, emergency managers need to provide requirements and program
definitions that can guide volunteer efforts towards addressing clearly-defined needs for the
greatest impact. Given a choice, the crisis crowd may want to support a defined project from the
Red Cross or local fire department than provide their time on a project of a perceived or
ambiguous need. During this time of budget and capacity challenges in the public sector, the
opportunity to encourage greater participation and support capacity is paramount. Today,

---

[1] Jenkins, Henry. *Confronting the Challenges of Participatory Culture: Media Education for the 21st Century.* Retrieved on the
Web from http://digitallearning.macfound.org/atf/cf/%7B7E45C7E0-A3E0-4B89-AC9C-

agencies and crisis response organizations have the ability to tap the "crisis crowd" which can potentially provide a significant realization of highly valuable skills and resources across all phases of emergency management spectrum.

In fact, our community, CrisisCommons, grew out of this need to connect technologies, open data and innovation with crisis response agencies and organizations before the crisis. During the Haiti earthquake, a group of technology volunteers gathered and asked ourselves, "What can we do to help?" Six months before we had created an open information-sharing and learning forum called CrisisCamp. Building on this idea, we rallied our networks to host CrisisCamps here in Washington DC and Mountain View, California. By January 15, 2010, five cities hosted CrisisCamps with another 14 cities seeking to create CrisisCamps the following weekend. Within 15 weeks, people around the world self-organized and collaborated with us to create 65 events in 8 countries in 30 cities with over 2,300 in-person registrations alone. A Haitian American filmmaker attending CrisisCamp in Los Angeles filmmaker shared why he was participating in the CrisisCamp movement[2]:

> *"The reason I came down was because I'm Haitian American and this is story that is very personal. My grandmother's brothers, some of them are in Haiti right now. Staying home and watching CNN, I couldn't just do that for another day or just look at the Internet or just give money, I felt like I need to volunteer -- to DO something."*

CrisisCamps were in-person gatherings where people pooled their skills and resources on projects efforts to support response activities. We learned there is great potential but we also found it challenging to put the full strength of everyones' capabilities and capacity to productive use; that was the hard part. While we had an abundance of human resources but we didn't have a good handle on the requirements needed by response agencies. In our CrisisCamp Haiti After Action Report[3], we found that we need to be able to (1) have relationships with response agencies who can provide requirements or problem definitions from the field, and (2) improve the ability to harness the productivity and value of people in a manner which enhances efforts, yet is not prescriptive, to allow for the greatest amount impact for the response and recovery.

Currently, crisis management structures and their overarching doctrine represent two opposing models: (1) The response model relies on the command and control structure which requires intensive training, knowledge of, and matriculation into "the system;" and (2) the recovery model requires partnership building and trust to move communities towards a shared vision to work together to rebuild their community. These approaches now exist in separate policy frameworks, seed two different cultures and collaboration behaviors. Both models are fueled by pre-existing relationships which may not be feasible. These models and their doctrine stand as silos with little or no resources allocated for the emergency management practitioner community to provide for the ability to include emergent volunteers who provide value and support for unimagined needs, but are not part of the emergency response plan. This unrealized asset, who the emergency management practitioner community may not plan for, could provide value and support for unimagined needs with surge support of a local (sometimes global) communities.

---

[2] January 25, 2011, *Geeks for Haiti*. Current TV.. Retrieved via the Web at http://www.youtube.com/watch?v=_ACMpgy7ce0
[3] December 2, 2010, *CrisisCamp After Action Report*. Retrieved via the Web at
http://wiki.crisiscommons.org/wiki/CrisisCamp_Haiti_AAR

Participatory crisis management can be defined as an open forum for participation by organizations, communities and networks of all kinds to actively support the preparedness of, response to, recovery from and mitigation against crisis events, especially at the local level. Today, we are starting to see some emergency management practitioners seek greater participation by the public, including volunteer technology communities (VTC), to support all aspects of crisis management.

"Participatory crisis management, to me as an emergency manager, is to actively engage the Citizen with preparedness, mitigation, and response information. What does the Citizen need to know to get through the crisis? How will the Citizen learn what is needed to engage for their recovery? It is important because, as we experienced in Hurricane Katrina, the Citizen is ill-prepared to activate their own survival and, in some cases, failed to heed the information being provided to them."
    - Lloyd Colston, City of Altus Emergency Management, Oklahoma

"The greater the participation across all sectors and social strata -- the more aware our society will be aware of the risks that we face."
    - Alex Rose, American Red Cross, Los Angeles, California

"Given the real time communication tools and networks now available to the general public, the public is now sharing crisis information, requests and resources online, in real time. Altruism and the need to validate information are strong drivers, made even more powerful and compelling with today's technology. As a result, current crisis management communication practices are no longer practical or as effective. Citizens are sharing information about what is happening in crisis even before the first responders arrive. In other words, crisis managers are behind from the "get go" in critical high profile events. We no longer "manage" crisis information. We "monitor", "correct", "disseminate", "survey" and "engage". Current crisis response policies and protocols do not adequately address the pressures and capabilities enabled by public use of social media tools in crisis. The National Incident Management System (NIMS) implementation and training guidance needs to be swiftly updated to reflect reality. It can't happen fast enough."
    - Bill Boyd, Bellingham Fire Department, Washington State

"Coming from 44 years from Civil Defense, through Red Cross, RACES, military, DOJ, DHS the community and National interests are only served through an inclusionary process, often missing. If it lives on any one's tax dollars, it needs to play nice. Vetting participants is important but no more important than inclusion of the volunteer / non-paid community. Liability law needs to support (these activities)."
- Everett Batey, Volunteer, ACS, VOAD, Lions Club, Oxnard, California

Following the Indian Ocean Tsunami, the United Nations moved toward a 'cluster system' to create greater inclusion in the response and recovery process. We would look towards this kind of cluster approach in guiding the creation of a national participatory crisis management system, which would be a collective of groups and individuals working together in an open and cooperative process. While there are challenges in this model, a cluster system designed around the participatory culture could sit alongside the current Emergency Support Function structure, and become a dynamic rallying point where response agencies could onboard new actors in a team environment. These teams, or affiliated networks, would plan for new actors and be able to channel individual skills and resources towards a common mission. It's not enough to have the National Response Framework with Emergency Support Functions, we also need an open and inclusive collaboration structure for stakeholders who emerge during a crisis and desire to help the response efforts. An inclusive cluster approach can serve to focus after action reporting, best practice development and continuous improvement regardless of the players involved across the emergency management spectrum including preparedness, response, recovery and mitigation.

In closing, we at CrisisCommons worked in an open and collaborative environment to development of our testimony, statement of record and our response to the questions for the record. Contributions and edits were made by people all over the world with a diverse skills and backgrounds.

2. You have direct FEMA experience. Can you share your perspectives on working with FEMA during and after disasters? (See also Attachment A)

Response: I had direct collaboration experience with FEMA while I worked for the U.S. Department of Homeland Security's Office of the Secretary and had in various roles including Public Liaison Officer and Deputy Director of the Ready Campaign within the Office of Public Affairs. I was also a Business Liaison of the Private Sector Office within the Office of Policy and worked on issues such as cybersecurity, incident management and business preparedness. This work included interaction and collaboration with industry sectors, such as technology and telecommunications. In my time at DHS, I supported my office's contribution to such policy documents as the National Response Framework (NRF) and the National Disaster Recovery Framework (NDRF).

Beyond my daily duties, I supported my particular office's incident planning, exercise and response needs. I have provided an overview of my experience (see Attachment A) during Hurricane Ike at the Joint Field Office. There were several opportunities and challenges that I experienced during my deployment:

- **Chain of Command:** As much as Chain of Command has its place in crisis response, there is an atmosphere at FEMA, and especially at the Joint Field Office, where "acting outside your box" or "providing creative problem solving" is not as encouraged. The response is heavily focused on reporting at every level for products which can be up to 12 hours old when finally "approved through the chain of command." Often the information is shared in a closed system, (ex. HSIN) or through a document based approach via PDF instead of a data feed.
- **Limitations of NRF Annex Roles:** I felt the effects and priority of how the NRF's "Annex" roles operate in the field verses ESF's. Additionally, there was the challenge of grouping mission space for a seamless response. However, this did not occur in all ESFs, and especially coordination of "Annex" functions. For example, CI/KR and private sector related agencies and organizations did not seem to work together. Perhaps the best model which reflected participatory culture within the JFO was in ESF-6 Mass Care where their leads created a collaborative group which coordinated mass care needs (similar to a cluster approach) which

was an inclusive body where any agency who was involved could participate. To my surprise, during Hurricane Ike this was the first time this has happened. Developing an inclusive body, was a best practice which could also be mirrored with online engagement. Looking at the future needs and capacity which Technology (including social media) can play, this is a consideration for any new element to the response structure. Some of the more important roles in crisis response are filled by those who operate under "Annexes" such as Critical Infrastructure, Volunteer Management and the Private Sector.

- **Individual-Based Deployment:** I was perplexed by the individual approach to response versus a more collaborative team based deployment. Additionally, the firewall blocked many programs and many of the Disaster Assistance Employees (DAE) came into the response with blank laptops which had no contacts or data. Many DAEs may have not local to the area. This is a potential challenge for future information sharing.
- **Dependence on Email.** The dependence on email is debilitating and unrealistic tool to effectively share information. This is its own "information overload" crisis within the actual crisis. The deluge of email and the dependence on "getting on the right email distribution list" hampers and distracts the ability of response personnel to focus their energy on "doing" rather than trying to keep up with "responding to email."
- **Limited Alternative Access to the Internet:** This perhaps is an opportunity for the greatest amount of improvement through partnership and corporate citizenship activities. During Hurricane Ike there were telecommunications companies that provided access to the Internet and cell phones within shelters. This challenge dates back to Hurricane Katrina as Humanity Road, an volunteer technology community, outlines in Attachment D. We see that not all shelters have provision for these resources. If FEMA requires the public to use a phone or a Web site in order to submit claims, for instance, then there could (or even should be) a provision for alternative access to use those tools in the shelters or other central locations. This would help ensure that the affected community is able to connect with disaster information and assistance.

2. (Continued) What missions and functions within FEMA could be enhanced by social media tools and information?

Response: FEMA's mission is to support our citizens and first responders to ensure that as a nation we work together to build, sustain, and improve our capability to prepare for, protect against, respond to, recover from, and mitigate all hazards. In review of the FEMA organization chart there is not one clear function focuses on the use of technology by citizens and emergency management to make the necessary actionable improvements to save lives and property during a crisis event. Each and every office has the ability to benefit from the use of social media tools and information. We would argue that social media and information is only one part of the spectrum. Data, digital literacy and collaborative systems could be part of how FEMA keeps up with the rapidly changing technology landscape. The application of technology and data vary depending on how people use them and how they are incorporated in the business processes of the agency. We can't stress this enough, technology is not the problem, the problem is that we need people to be trained and to be empowered to take the risk to innovate how FEMA (and the emergency management system) does business. Technology is the tool; but the people and data the power these technologies represent that are the most important institutional investment.

In specific respect to FEMA's organization, we see technology capability working across the agency, with specific support for preparedness, mitigation, response and recovery. As much as we can be prescriptive on how this inclusion could work within each particular mission space, we feel an evaluation, resource and skill mapping would need to occur to survey what exists, identify gaps and to allow for emergency management practitioner and public input. We have outlined a few critical areas such as operations, preparedness and product development, that we believe should be at the top priorities:

Opportunity to Support FEMA Operations

During the National Level Exercise (NLE) 2011, CrisisCommons was introduced and became a member of the ESF-5 Situational Assessment Working Group. During this time, we worked with the Social Media in Emergency Management (SMEM) Initiative which is a global community of emergency management practitioners who share best practices and lessons learned in using social media in the emergency management profession. Through this open engagement a small team provided recommended injects added to the NLE Master Scenerio Events Lists (MSEL) and the Whole of Community approach to the exercise. The SMEM team developed three potential Courses of Action (See Attachment B) for the exercises and weighed their risks and benefits. The following were key findings from the group shared with FEMA's NLE Team:

- **Need for a Technology Cluster which has liaisons within each ESF.** NIMS needs to be updated to fully incorporate the use of data (especially data from non-traditional sources such as social media) Since this data is needed by decision-makers, the reporting structure could have a component of a Special Advisor (leadership level) who would act as a liaison to the leadership of the incident. This position should be replicated at all levels of government; local, State and Federal. This entity would have external collaboration functions with the private sector and with volunteer technology communities.
- **Need for a User Defined/Dynamic Operational Picture.** This is done for information at each level, local, state national, NGO, etc. Often we believe that interoperability is about movement of data, one system to another, where instead interoperability could be about access to the right data. Moving data increases complexity as well as digital liability including the requirements of storage and maintenance. However, our approach would allow each operational unit to store and maintain their own data which would provide an ability to question datasets so to only move and manage what is critical and/or required. Each unit can determine what information they need for their operational picture with teh ability to answer questions.
- **Need for Data Identification, Categorization & Planning.** Need for a data interoperability matrix or planning document used to identify data sources. The document should include: EEI's, format, location, access control, security and other metadata as needed by a Technology Action Team (as part of the Technology Cluster) to expedite the use of common data sets between responding organizations.
- **Need for Data Preparedness.** Defining and making available data needed by emergency management before the crisis. Making data searchable, findable and more available (shareable).
- **Need to add a focus on data sets** provided in and through open information and social networks. This has been the data unavailable and/or unobtainable to entities involved in

the disaster. We recommend there be a data coordinator to provide the ability to determine a nexus, filtering and other data support processes between public and private data.

During planning for the NLE 11, one of the continual discussions centered on the concept of "Commons Operating Picture." There was much interest in our group regarding the need for this concept to be redefined and goals reset to encourage the availability of data and its consumption and not a systems-based "we have to have it one place" approach. Our group understood, based on extensive experience, that an incident commander in the field has a different data needs than the Administrator of FEMA. Both need to have access, but the way in which they use it, visualize it and make decisions from that data will be different.

With regards to the inclusion of social media from an operational perspective, there was wasn't a clear position or role on who would support that engagement during a crisis and work to provide continuous improvement during steady state. Often social media is regulated to a Public Affairs function within the Joint Information Center. But during the first 48 hours public information abut the crisis can be some of the best sources of situational awareness information, as was witnessed in the aftermath from the Japanese earthquake where people shared video and images almost real-time from the scene.

A significant challenge today the use of *social media, data and other information activities rarely are captured in lessons learned or after action reporting*. It is imperative that these lessons be documented. Without this knowledge, it is challenging for practitioners to justify resources or build policy to support mission objectives. In the initial findings of the Social Media in Emergency Management Camp[4], emergency practitioners described how creating "buy-in" within their own organization is a significant challenge. Often social media and other technology related activities are championed not by management rather by the practitioners who often take on risk to explore new and innovative approaches to support their mission.

Opportunity to Increase Our Nation's Digital Preparedness

FEMA has an opportunity to encourage digital preparedness by the emergency management practitioner community and of the public. Today, we are ever dependent on mobile technologies, but often don't know how to effectively use them in a crisis event. For example, on Facebook's platform, it would be helpful to share with citizens, perhaps in local partnerships with emergency management, how they can text their Facebook status updates to let their friends and family know "I'm Okay." This simple action may create a better chance that their update will reach their friends and family, rather than making a voice call or trying to pull up a web application on their mobile phones, both of which use needed bandwidth during a time when everyone wants to connect with family and loved ones. We know that after a crisis, cell phone towers get overwhelmed, but texting to social networks could lower bandwidth needed to get a message through in a crisis. This is the kind of information companies like Facebook, Twitter, Microsoft and Google, even hardware providers like Apple and telecommunications carriers like AT&T and Verizon could provide their customers which could help the people who depend on their

---

[4] Social Media in Emergency Management Camp Initial Findings. (2011) Retrieved on July 7, 2011 at http://www.cna.org/sites/default/files/news/2011/SMEM11_InitialFindings.pdf

products. A significant opportunity exists to enhance many of the private sectors' public safety and education information.

Opportunity to Infuse Public Safety Considerations in Social Media and other Technologies

FEMA, and emergency management practitioners across the country, are making investments and decisions based on today's state of technology. However, we don't know how challenging this is for the first responder community. Emergency managers and practitioners have shared that they don't know "where to go to see 'what's out there' without being sold a product." There are many emergency managers and practitioners who are innovators themselves. Their voices need to be heard. We need to encourage the private sector and open source communities to build tools and systems which are collaborative in nature (extending the utility) and take into account the business of crisis that FEMA is in everyday.

On June 7, 2011 CrisisCommons was invited to a meeting with Facebook's new Disaster Relief Workgroup[5]. This was an exploratory meeting where Facebook's platform team was interested in talking about where they fit and how they could add value in during crisis events. During the meeting, several crisis response agencies voiced concern that they need assistance such as verified pages and explained the challenges of recycled (i.e., old) information during a crisis. During crisis events it's often hard to see what information may be from a response agency verses a community unaffiliated with the response.

Ideally to meet FEMA's mission, these conversations need to be held in an open forum, would be a permanent ongoing process between emergency management practitioner community, crisis response organizations, volunteer technology communities and owners and operators of private sector technology platforms and open source communities. This engagement is not only valuable for building relationships, but for improving the ability of the public to access and potentially act on emergency information.

Going a step further, public safety considerations could be "baked in" to the development and training of these platforms to the public. Additionally, it would be helpful for the purveyors of these platforms to educate the emergency management community on how to use these tools and to share trends of about how people are using crisis information and new social behaviors which these tools support. For example, Facebook recently released a new way to geolocate a person's status update. This has both a city and state option, but it doesn't have a county option. For agencies like the National Weather Service or FEMA and the county's themselves, having a county option may be helpful. Perhaps, the county option wasn't something Facebook considered because its is not necessarily their job to understand how crisis information is distributed and shared. This is why companies, such as Facebook, could benefit from a public safety advisors who could provide input on feature and product development. Ideally when the product is in its concept phase throughout production. There is a potential to utilize FEMA's National Advisory Council in this role. There could be a new Technology Committee established where public safety, private sector, open source communities and volunteer technology communities can come together to explore opportunities and challenges across the emergency management spectrum, including innovation and product development.

---

[5] Blanchard, Heather. *Big Ideas for Facebook Disaster Relief.* (June 9, 2011). Retrieved at http://crisiscommons.org/2011/06/09/big-ideas-for-facebook-disaster-relief/

Turning to long term investment and modernization of our nation's emergency response system, resources such as a National Academies/Computer Science and Telecommunications Board study (See Attachment C) could lay out a long-term forward-looking vision for using information technology for federal emergency management and develop a roadmap for computer systems and infrastructure modernization. It would review the current state of technical infrastructure and systems architecture and current plans for its evolution, and make recommendations to FEMA and its partners on modernizing business and information processes, practices, and information systems to meet today's and tomorrow's demands, including how to build in the flexibility to cope with changing requirements and usage models. It would also consider the financial and human resources necessary to implement this modernization. A consensus report setting forth the Council's recommendations could be issued.

In a sense this kind of challenge starts a new conversation. Is there an obligation to ensure that the public is informed on how to use proprietary and open source consumer technology products in a crisis? Do they know (or share their findings) of how the public uses their product in a crisis? Currently, with regard to Facebook, only the company knows how people are using their platform. Those findings and trend data can draw attention and insights on how public safety can improve their digital engagement and be prepared to fully utilize the public as a resource during a crisis.

a. Do you believe the necessary liaison role between volunteer organizations and the government can be fulfilled by an existing position at DHS, or would this necessitate the creation of a new position?

Response: At CrisisCommons, we believe there isa critical need to have a liaison role between volunteer technology communities (VTC) and government at all levels, including FEMA. This was a major finding for CrisisCommons response activities. We believe there is a need for requirements to be delineated from response agencies to the VTCs. Once VTCs understand what is needed they could then provide mutual assistance and surge capacity and support a "Whole of Community" approach to the response and recovery effort. Without requirements from response agencies and other affiliated response organizations, VTCs are marginalized and have little ability to identify and provide productive and constructive support activities. There is the old adage, "the time to exchange business cards is before disaster." This concept also applies to technology and data. We learned from the Haiti response effort that during a crisis is not the time to implement new business process or technology tools that are not used both by either headquarters and/or field elements. We do see a great need for initiative and empowerment within emergency management to harness their ability to work with VTCs and other external actors to problem solve to fill unanticipated just-in-time needs.

At FEMA authority and resource allocation are paramount. It is not enough just to create a liaison to VTCs without authority to act or resources critical to accomplishing their mission. If FEMA is to begin to build long-term capacity, harness the full capability of technology resources and skills within the federal government, and provide support to our nation's emergency management practitioners, it must invest not only in systems, but in the people and business processes required to meet the rise of the networked information economy and the exponential growth and availability of data to inform decision makers and resource allocation. Resources and authorities for emergency response authorities to use social media tools, the the training that is necessary are critical elements and gaps which must be filled today and provide a path ahead for long term capacity and capability improvement.

"Another way FEMA could be helpful would be to support emergency management agencies in acquiring tools, training & education in social media through grant programs like EMPG. Currently, "approved" communications include alert & warning technologies like EAS and community notification systems, but everyday technologies are often not supported as EM activities. Legitimizing social media would validate its use and promoting training & exposure will be key for senior emergency managers."
- Cheryl Bledsoe, Clark County Emergency Management, Washington State

We recommend that this critical role be closely connected, even defined, by state and local response agencies and the Federal Interagency. The role cannot create in a vacuum; it must be facilitated through an open process which allows for the greatest amount of inclusion and input. There is a danger in only looking inward and setting up to "fight the last war." This critical role, and its greater Office, have to be fluent not only in today's technology, but also in tomorrow's, similar to what is required of commercial technology and telecommunications industries. The personnel in these roles have to be able to act with agility, be located where the technology innovation is happening and have special authorities to allow for engagement and innovation -- which may require risk taking.

a. (Continued) Please provide a recommendation for where this position could be housed and what the reporting structure could look like.

Response: CrisisCommons recommends that this position be housed as branch of a new FEMA Office of Technology Innovation and Adoption. This office could bring together existing capabilities and advise the FEMA Administrator and be his counsel on the future direction of technology, including social media, open data initiatives, geospatial activities, open source software development and incident management. This office could also provide insights across FEMA's leadership including the FEMA Chief Information Officer. Below is a concept of this office and just a few of the priorities it could support.

Figure 1. Reporting within the FEMA Structure

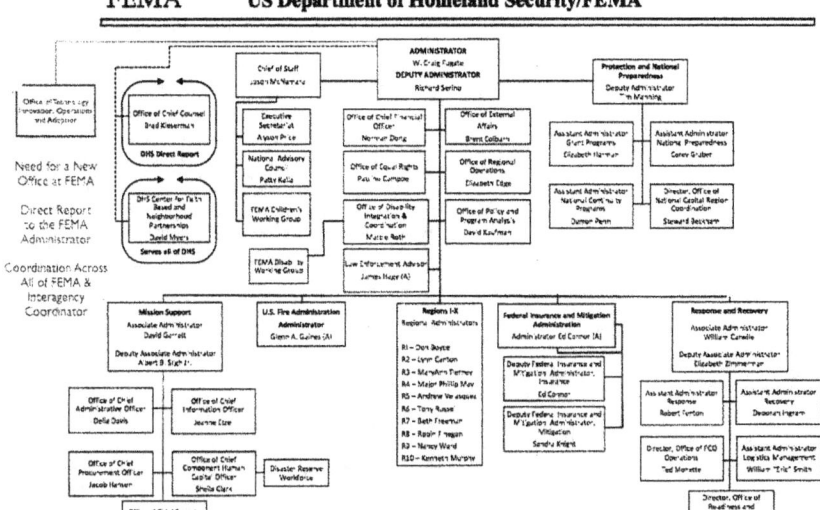

H605-41331-79W7 with DISTILLER

Figure 2. Proposed Steady-State Conceptual Approach

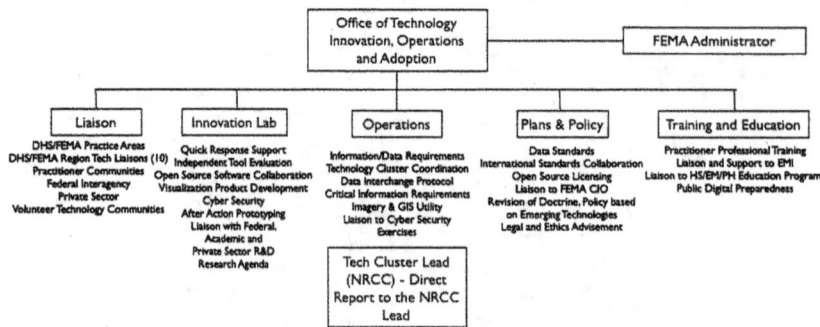

**Figure 3. Potential Incorporation into the
National Incident Command System**

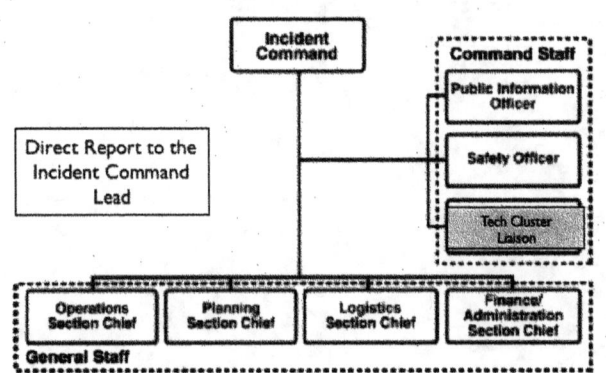

Figure 4. Potential Incorporation into the Joint Field Office

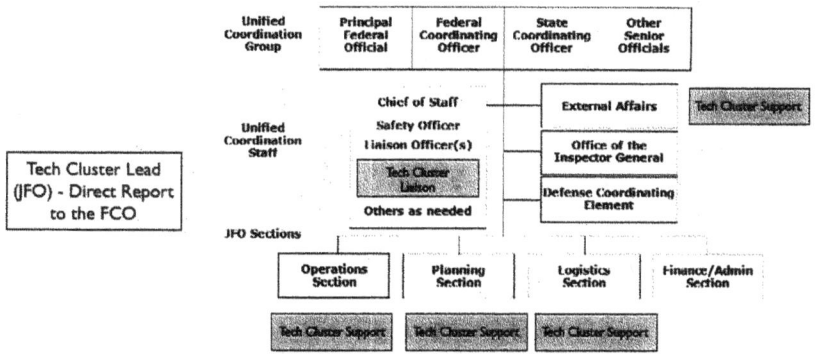

Figure 5. Potential Framework for an Technology Cluster (Operations) Within the NRCC or any Emergency Operations Center

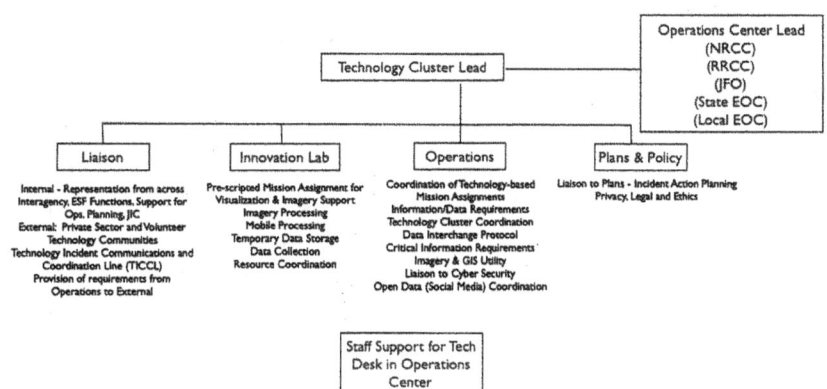

122

**Figure 6. Potential Operational Framework for Technology Cluster
Volunteer Technology Liaison to the Greater Volunteer Technology Communities**

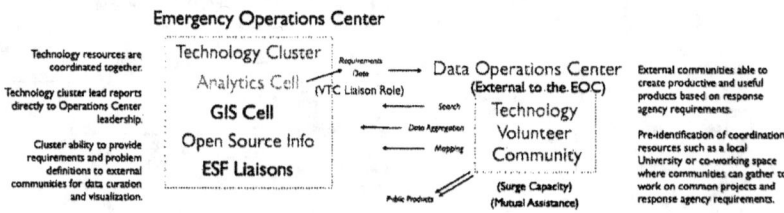

Æ

www.ingramcontent.com/pod-product-compliance
Lightning Source LLC
Chambersburg PA
CBHW052000280526
45793CB00005B/799